Cemetery

Crypt

Refugee
school

School

R. Glane

trance

Execution sites

To LIMOGES

ORADOUR
Village of the dead

ORADOUR
Village of the dead

PHILIP BECK

Leo Cooper
London

To Marie-Cécile
who went there with me
and was equally moved.

First Published in Great Britain 1979 by
Leo Cooper Ltd
196 Shaftesbury Avenue, London WC2H 8JL

Copyright © 1979 by Philip Beck

ISBN 0 85052 252 8

Designed by John Mitchell
Printed and bound in Great Britain at
The Pitman Press, Bath

Contents

Acknowledgments

The author acknowledges with thanks the advice and help he received from Dr. R. Lapuelle (Mayor of Oradour), Monsieur A. Hivernaud, Monsieur and Madame Lamaud, Monsieur J. Hourrière, Monsieur Claude Levy of the *Comité d'Histoire de la 2ème Guerre Mondiale*, and Miss J. Carmichael of the Imperial War Museum.

The author and publisher are also grateful to the authors and publisher of *Oradour sur Glane, Vision d'Epouvante* for permission to reproduce the photographs on pp. 21, 25, 26, 27, 28, 32 and 45, to Keystone Press Agency Ltd for the photographs on pp. 75 and 78, and to the Bundesarchiv for the photograph on p. 53.

The jacket photographs are reproduced by kind permission of the Robert Hunt Picture Library.

Boris Weltman drew the maps.

Preface

On 10 June, 1944, four days after the Allied landing in Normandy, while the attention of the world was focused on the progress of the battle, a crime was committed by the Waffen SS hundreds of miles away in central France which must be unique in the history of that army of ruthless killers. 642 men, women and children were killed in the village of Oradour-sur-Glane, near Limoges. The SS burned every building, leaving behind, as they rolled away in the evening, ruins filled with the stench of burnt human flesh.

This mixed band of butchers—many of them were not Germans—was composed mainly of men between the ages of 17 and 25. That night they drank and sang with apparent unconcern in the village in which they were billeted.

One of them was overheard boasting to his companion, 'I killed 26 of them.'

There have been several versions of what actually happened on that dreadful day and many theories about the motive for the slaughter. In fact, it is the enigma 'Why Oradour?' which has been one of the main spurs to my research.

I am convinced that the people of Oradour did nothing to provoke their appalling fate. In fact, I believe that, had it not been for the extraordinary carelessness and impatience of one man, unconnected with the village, the massacre would not have occurred.

Subsequent research may prove otherwise, but I believe that, on the facts at present available, this story is as near the truth as anyone can get today.

An aerial view of the old village with the Church in the foreground.

The new Oradour.

1 The Ruins

A signpost pointing to Oradour-sur-Glane on Route Nationale 147 between Poitiers and Limoges probably means nothing to the average holidaymaker on the way to Spain or the South of France. There is no tourist sign reading:

> ORADOUR-SUR-GLANE
> (*Village Martyr*)
> *Ses ruines*
> *Son église tragique*
> *Son cimetière*
> *Son nouveau village*

Following a map, I branched off to the right a short distance from Limoges. I travelled for a surprising distance along country lanes and had the impression that the place didn't want to be visited. At a crossroads the only indication was a hand-painted piece of board almost hidden in the hedge. I was beginning to think I had missed it. Then suddenly there was the ruined village on a gentle slope above a tree-girt river.

I had first read of the tragedy about ten years before. There had been an article in the French News magazine, *Match*, with pictures. I was astonished that I had never heard of it before. I read that the ruins had been preserved and they became an obsession. I had to visit them. I even dreamt about them. I imagined I flew over them. They were black and grey and frightening. The new Oradour adjoining was full of life and neon signs.

Reality presented two immediate surprises—the warm colour of the

1

The entrance to the ruins.

ruins, an ochre intensified by the evening sun, and the proximity of the church to the main entrance. I had always visualized it at the far end of the village.

The new village, off to the left, was a characterless, concrete huddle dominated by a squat church with a square, lighthouse-type tower.

To anyone who doesn't know the dreadful story the ruins may seem little more than a curiosity. They are enclosed by a low wall and have three gated entrances which are locked at night. At each entrance there is a sign which reads simply: *Souviens-Toi—Remember*. At the main entrance another sign requests that visitors should be correctly attired, conduct themselves with decorum, not go into the houses and keep dogs on leads.

The first group of ruined houses on the right, flanking a pleasant green with trees, bears the notice 'Silence'.

There is no commercialism of the style which mars Mont St Michel, Lourdes and other tourist centres. Entrance is free and there is only one discreet stall, just inside the gates, where appropriate literature and a few postcards are on sale.

The roofless church, which once had a steeple, dominates the main

entrance. It was the scene of the worst act of the tragedy—the slaughter of hundreds of women and children whose screams were heard for miles around.

One can see the window, identified by a tablet, from which Madame Rouffanche, the sole survivor, escaped. The grille which once covered it is still bent outwards, marking the passage of her body.

There is a larger tablet near the main entrance which tells what happened in the church. It has been fixed to the wall near a crucifix which, says the inscription, remained unscathed.

The main street, Rue Emile Desourteaux—a familiar Oradour name, as will be seen—is still bordered on the right, as one ascends between the ruined houses, by the tramlines which linked the village with

Limoges and other villages. The roofless tram station where the line branches into two tracks is about midway up the street.

The tramway was opened in 1911 and was a great boon to the villagers because, apart from its transport, it provided electricity and street lighting for the village.

As one progresses through the ruins a feeling of desolation is augmented by one of a sudden extinction of life, as at Pompeii. The whole population, apart from a few who miraculously got away after the SS arrived, died there during one afternoon. They were taken from their homes in that picturesque village—even in ruins it is far more attractive than the new village—just after lunch on 10 June, 1944 and herded to their deaths.

In the ruined kitchens are saucepans, frying pans, coffee grinders and other utensils. Garages contain the rusty wrecks of cars. Fire-buckled bicycles hang from nails on walls. No one had a chance to escape.

Many houses contain rusty sewing machines, some of which seem to have been purposely placed on window sills to underline the industry of their dead owners. Frankly I'm surprised that, in these days of widespread vandalism and in view of the cynicism of the young towards the ruins, so many of these items remain. No doubt over the years some have been lifted as souvenirs.

The Champ de Foire, the village green where the population was assembled by the SS, is on the right of the main street going up. It must have been a delightful place before the disaster, with its varied architecture, trees and covered well. Now it is bordered by the empty shells of houses, one of which bears a plaque telling of the assembly.

On the grass lie the rusty remains of the car which belonged to the village doctor who arrived back from his rounds just as the round-up had been completed. He joined the others.

Across the green lie the memorial grounds. A wide, hedged lawn leads to a bench-like arrangement of stones on the roof of a crypt.

The crypt contains stone tablets bearing the names and ages of all the victims. In side chambers are glass-topped cases set in stone which hold personal possessions found among the charred human remains—wed-

Dr Desourteaux's car.

ding rings and other jewellery, watches, pocket knives, a cigarette case pierced by a bullet, a denture, etc. Most have been distorted by fire.

Beyond lies the cemetery, dominated by a column which marks the communal grave of most of the population whose remains were unidentifiable. The flat stone bears two glass-topped coffins in which one can see collections of blue-grey, charred human bone fragments. This, to my mind, is a vulgar, unnecessary display.

The most pitiful sight is, of course, the family tombs bearing photographs of the dead. Whole families are pictured with inscriptions after their names indicating that they were 'killed', 'massacred' or 'burned' by the 'Nazis' or 'Germans' on 10 June, 1944.

Some of them bear plastic or china flowers. Some are garish and blatant in their silent expression of grief. The more discreet—such as a plain stone with a single picture of a pretty girl embedded in it and a

caption giving only her name and date of death—are the most impressive.

Six tablets in various parts of the village identify the buildings in which the men were shot. Each bears the notice: *Ici Lieu de Supplice. Un Groupe D'Hommes Fut Massacré et Brûlé par les Nazis. Recueillez-vous**. (Place of execution. A group of men were massacred and burnt by the Nazis.) There are barns, garages and a smithy. In some, bullet holes can be seen in the brickwork.

A large barn in the *Rue du Cimetière* is identified as the place from which six men escaped,—the only survivors of the fusillades which killed 190 men. Five of them got through a hole in a door at the rear after playing dead. The sixth tried another way out and was later found shot dead, halfway through a fence.

There is a tablet outside a gutted bakery—one can still distinguish the

---

* Not an easy word to translate. It means roughly 'compose yourself' (to prayer).

la MÉMOIRE de nos Chères FILLETTES et ...EUR...
Ravies à Notre Affecti...

AUDINE   RENÉE   HUGUETTE   MARYSE
3 ans   10 ans   7 ans   6 ans

...lèves de l'Ecole d'ORADOUR-sur-GLANE
Massacrées et brûlées dans l'Eglise,
Par les hordes nazies, le 10 Juin 1944.

ICI
LIEU DE SUPPLICE
UN GROUPE D'HOMMES FUT
MASSACRÉ ET BRÛLÉ PAR LES NAZIS
RECUEILLEZ – VOUS

word *Boulangerie* over the shop window—telling that human remains were found in the rusty ovens one can see inside. A farmyard well is identified as the tomb of a number of unknown people.

In the gardens at the rear of the houses are the wells, many still holding water. There was no piped water in the village so there are privies, mostly two-seaters, at the bottom of the gardens.

An untended vine climbs a dead wall outside a roofless bathroom which still has its iron bath. A rusty gate into a lane has been pierced by bullets. Several people were found hiding in their gardens and shot on the spot.

Some of the houses bear tablets commemorating their inhabitants. One in black marble with gold lettering ends its inscription with the single word REMENBER. Another, fixed to the ruins of the home of the Mayor, Dr Jean Desourteaux, and his son, Dr Jacques Desourteaux, has been contributed by the *Association Amicale des Médecins du Maquis et de la Résistance.*

The most awe-inspiring sight is, of course, the interior of the church. It is calm and open to the skies. Yet anyone with any degree of sensitivity must surely feel the atmosphere and visualize the terrible scene that occurred there.

There is a battered pram before the damaged altar—a symbol of the many in which babies soon to be slaughtered were wheeled into the church by their frightened mothers.

On the right, as one faces the altar, is the little door against which a pile of burnt bodies was found. On the left, next to the altar, is the door to the vestry which was burst open by frantic, screaming women and children trying to get away from the asphyxiating fumes of the smoke grenades the SS placed in the choir. That door has been replaced and is locked. The vestry floor, which must have been wooden, has gone.

The window through which Madame Rouffanche made her escape is directly behind the altar. In the left transept is a chapel with a small altar which is less damaged. Behind it is a wooden confessional which miraculously escaped damage by the flames. Yet the heat was so intense that it melted the bells which are now nothing more than a mass of distorted bronze near the main entrance.

The bakery in which two bodies were found in the ovens.

A uniformed guide with a strong local accent tells the story to the curious visitor. The place is kept locked when he is not around.

The ruins comprise a total of 254 buildings. They have been preserved as a unique and impressive monument to the dead. But not everyone agrees with the idea. Young people tend to regard the ruins with disdain. Someone had defaced the notice at the main entrance with a paint spray, writing *Oubliez* (forget) over it.

In fact, many people think the ruins should have been rebuilt. The Germans offered to do this after the war. Others feel that Oradour should have been restored with the exception of the church and the places where the men were shot. It would certainly have been a more attractive village than the new Oradour. That uninspired collection of buildings has been built round a main street called *Avenue du 10 Juin*. The side streets are simply named *Rue Numero Un, Rue Numero Deux*, etc. However, I suppose that's better than *Rue des Martyrs, Rue du Supplice*, etc.

The new village was completed in 1953 but, as the Mayor told me, it took years to achieve full occupation, which is understandable. The establishment of two factories helped to attract residents. However, there were many disputes over inheritance rights. In so many cases direct heirs had died and distant cousins turned up to claim their inheritance.

I was amazed to hear that Madame Rouffanche still lived there, in a little house near the Town Hall. She was over 80. It seemed strange that she should want to live within sight of a scene of such indescribable horror and tragedy in her life. Perhaps she wanted to be near the remains of her lost family. Perhaps she had nowhere else to go.

2 The Massacre

On Saturday, 10 June, 1944, Oradour-sur-Glane was unusually full. The population had been swollen by a number of refugees, including many from Alsace-Lorraine, and people had come in from neighbouring hamlets and farms to do their shopping and collect their tobacco ration which was distributed every ten days.

There were also visitors from Limoges in search of food, which was more easily obtainable in the country, and a number of anglers hoping for sport in the River Glane.

Tragically there was a full attendance in the schools because there was to be a medical inspection and vaccination that afternoon. The boys' school, opposite the tram station, had a complement of 64 and the girls' school 106. The latter was divided into three classes, two being in a building on the main street near the Champ de Foire while the third, for infants, was on the road leading to the hamlet of Les Bordes. In the same road was a special school for children from Alsace-Lorraine.

A light-hearted mood prevailed. The only German soldiers ever seen in the village had been a few officers who had come to dine at the hotels. There was talk of troop movements in the region, particularly at St Junien, six miles away, but no convoys were expected. Most of the talk was about the landings in Normandy. The people believed that at long last the end of the German occupation was in sight.

It was the eve of a religious festival with a First Communion service and the interior of the little church had been decorated with flowers. There had been a light drizzle in the morning but at 2 o'clock the sky was clearing and the sun came through. In many homes the midday meal was late because the men had been working in the fields and had not long returned from a full morning's work.

The hotels were full and at that hour most of the guests were well into their meal or had ordered their coffee. At the Hotel Milord, which still had an excellent menu despite the food shortage, there were 20 people in one party. The visitors included some from as far away as Paris, a young pelota champion from Marseilles and a young woman who had returned to Oradour to pick up some silver and other values from her home there.

The guests at the Hotel Avril included a woman with her three children and her niece. She had taken refuge in Oradour from Paris where she feared there would be a bombardment.

There were several groups of 'foreigners' in the village. Between twenty and thirty Spaniards who had taken refuge from the civil war worked in Oradour as farm labourers, mechanics, chambermaids, etc. There was a Jewish family from Bordeaux living in the village under an assumed name.

A family named Lévignac who lived in Avignon, perturbed by the bombing in that town, had evacuated their sons, Serge (16) and Charles (12), to Oradour where they felt they would be safer. The elder boy was billeted with a farmer just outside the village while the younger lived with an 80-year-old woman and her daughter, who was nearly 60. Monsieur Lévignac arrived in Oradour on the 9th and stayed overnight in one of the hotels. He spent the Saturday morning with his sons, then took the tram to Limoges. He would be back in the afternoon. He sent a postcard to his wife in which he said, 'I feel I am giving our sons life itself'.

Also in the village that day were two sons of Professor Forest of Montpellier, a philosopher. He and his wife were natives of Oradour. Madame Forest's father, Monsieur Clavaud, aged 82, lived in the village with his second daughter and her husband, Monsieur and Madame Rousseau, who ran the boys' school.

Professor and Madame Forest had arrived in March to take up residence in a wing of the small manor house of Laplaud, on a wooded ridge 1½ kms west of Oradour, the home of their friend, the Vicomtesse de Saint-Venant.

They had six children, the eldest of whom was in a Maquis group in south-west France. The two who had walked into Oradour that day were Michel (20), who was studying law, and Dominique who was 6½. Michel was a poet and deeply religious. He kept a diary in which he had written at one time, 'I shall die young. But does it matter?'

The two often went for walks together. Dominique was a gentle, affectionate child and his father's favourite. He was going to take his First Communion in Oradour on 11 June and had to look his best. So he had gone to the village with his brother on Saturday to have his hair cut and visit his grandfather.

Professor Forest had gone to Limoges by tram, accompanied by his sons Jacques, Bernard and François.

A brother and sister from Strasbourg, Emile and Odile Neumeyer, were staying with Oradour's parish priest, the Abbé Chapelle, aged 70, who had been in the village for 33 years. He was poor and humble and had had to take care of himself since his aged housekeeper died.

The Abbé Chapelle had, since the war, been obliged to extend his ministry to Javerdat, about 5 km to the west. Despite his age, he walked there every morning, whatever the weather, to say Mass.

The Neumeyer family were, for a time, refugees, living at a house near the presbytery. When most of them decided to return to Strasbourg, Odile, who was 33, stayed behind to look after the priest. Her brother Emile went to a mission school at Cellule in the Auvergne. He had a brief holiday which started on 8 June. When he arrived at Oradour he found his sister ill so he helped the priest with the housework and to prepare for Sunday's important service. He also agreed to act as server at the Saturday Mass.

Bernadette Cordeau's father was doing forced labour in East Prussia. Bernadette, who was 16, lived with her mother at the home of her grandmother in Les Bordes, a hamlet a short distance to the north-east of Oradour. She went to Oradour to learn dressmaking; her mother worked as secretary to a doctor in Limoges.

On 10 June Madame Cordeau's employer was on call so she had to stay in Limoges overnight. She told Bernadette it would be best in the circumstances if she went to work in Oradour that day.

Denise Bardet, aged 24, was a teacher at the girls' school. She had accompanied some of her pupils to St Junien the day before to take an exam and had heard of the brutal behaviour of the SS in other parts of the region. St Junien had been invaded by an SS Regiment following the blowing-up of a viaduct near the town by the *Maquis*. Denise saw the armed soldiers and felt a sense of relief when she and her charges returned to peaceful Oradour on the bus with its charcoal-burning stove at the rear.

So far in the war Oradour had been a peaceful backwater. It was well away from the main routes of military traffic, and it had not been the scene of any *Maquis* activity. It was therefore with some surprise that people in the streets, particularly those at the lower end of the village, heard the rumble of heavy vehicles approaching from the direction of Limoges.

The people in the hotels and restaurants were too absorbed in their coffee and brandy, with full French conversational accompaniment, to notice the sound. It was the same in the schools where the children had not yet been called to order for the afternoon session.

It was exactly 2.15 pm when the SS arrived. As with the rest of the operations, everything was worked out to a time schedule. There were about a dozen vehicles in the convoy. Five of them—three lorries and two tracked vehicles—went straight up the main street almost to the end. There the latter turned round and came back down to the bridge over the Glane. Both ends of the main street were thus blocked while other vehicles quickly moved in to seal off the other exits.

The vehicles were packed with young soldiers wearing camouflage tunics and steel helmets with camouflaged canvas covers. They were heavily armed with rifles and machine guns. They jumped down as soon as their transport came to a halt and, under the barked orders of the NCOs, hurried to surround the entire village. When the operation had been completed a white flare was fired.

At first the people watched these manoeuvres with surprise and

14

Oradour before the massacre. The man in the foreground is standing on the site of the entrance to the ruins today.

interest, then with disquiet. What on earth was happening? Some thought it was part of the general retreat from the area by the occupation forces, in view of the battle in the north. Others anticipated a checking of identity papers—nothing more.

Monsieur Aimé Renaud, one of the few who escaped, said he felt uneasy from the very first and, meeting Monsieur Denis, a wine merchant, advised him to go and hide. The latter said he was not afraid of the Germans.

'They are just ordinary men like us,' he added. 'In any case I'm old and no longer afraid of anything.'

Martial Brissaud, aged 17, who had just arrived in the village from Les Bordes to visit a friend, was afraid he might be picked up and deported for forced labour. But the Mayor, Dr Jean Desourteaux, an elderly man with a white beard, and a teacher, Monsieur Rousseau, to whom he expressed his fears, tried to reassure him. There was really no need for panic. It was some sort of military manoeuvre which would soon be over.

But Martial was not convinced. He managed to evade the troops and got back to his home where he hid in the loft. He couldn't convince the other members of his family of the danger. He was the sole survivor. He was hiding in the fields when his home went up in flames.

A Jewish family was staying at the Hotel Avril. The parents told their children they would be arrested whatever happened and advised them to run away and hide. The two girls, of 18 and 22 and a boy, aged 9, hid under an outside staircase leading to the garden. They stayed there until the hotel caught fire. They crossed three gardens and were stopped by sentries who, after a brief argument among themselves, let them go.

Another Jew, a dentist named Levy from Rennes, was dining with Madame Jeanne Leroy from St Malo when the SS arrived. His wife was in a concentration camp and he had no papers. He immediately fled and hid in the fields all day. Madame Leroy stayed, believing there would only be an identity check. She had been obliged to leave her flat in St Malo in 1942 when the Todt organization took over the whole building. She had rented a house near Rennes, but, fearing there might be fighting

The Champ de Foire.

in that area when the second front opened, took a friend's advice and move to Oradour in April, 1944.

The Mayor was summoned by the officer commanding the SS. The town crier, Monsieur Depierrefiche, was sent out accompanied by two soldiers to beat his drum and announce that the whole population was to assemble at the Champ de Foire immediately, bringing their identity papers.

So it was after all only an identity check. There was momentary relief. But when the soldiers started hustling the people out of their homes, beating open locked doors with rifle butts and generally acting in a brutal manner, fear began to mount.

No one was spared from the round-up. A wounded war veteran who could not move quickly enough was beaten and shoved along the street. Elderly people were also treated roughly. Every house was entered and the occupants evacuated—if they had not already left—with no account being taken of age or infirmity.

A school teacher, Madame Andrée Binet, who was ill in bed, was made to get up and given no time to dress. She arrived at the Champ de Foire in a dressing gown. A baker appeared stripped to the waist and covered with flour. A man who had been in the chair at the barber's shop had not been given time to remove the white gown and was half-shaved.*

Lorries packed with people who had been picked up in the neighbourhood started to arrive. Men had been removed from the fields, women and children from the farmhouses and cottages. They were very scared and many were weeping.

In fact the scenes in the countryside around Oradour must have been as dramatic as those in the village.

The Belivier family who lived at Les Brégères saw the SS men running towards their farmhouse. Madame Belivier's instant reaction was to tell her 18-year-old son Marcel to go and hide because she feared he would be taken for deportation. Like Martial Brissaud, he emerged from his hiding place in the fields in the evening to find his home had been destroyed and his parents were missing.

The Rouffanche family lived at La Ferme de l'Etang. They comprised Jean and Marguerite with their children Jean, Amélie and Andrée. Amélie was a young married woman with a daughter of seven months.

The family had just finished their lunch and Jean Rouffanche was preparing to return to his work on the land with his children who helped him run the farm. Marguerite was to stay and look after her grandchild. Suddenly the SS burst in and ordered them to go to Oradour at once with their identity papers. Amélie put her child in its pram. On the road outside they were joined by neighbouring families.

The schools were invaded almost simultaneously. The children were

* This was Monsieur Broussaudier, one of the survivors of the shooting of the men.

18

told to assemble outside and follow the soldiers to the Champ de Foire. There was great excitement. It was an unexpected break from school routine and promised to be an interesting one. Only the teachers were apprehensive, but they tried not to show it. They told some of the children they were going to have a group photograph taken. The little ones were promised sweets.

In one school the teacher had just written on the blackboard for copying the sentence: '*Je prends la resolution de ne jamais faire de mal aux autres.*' (I resolve never to do ill to others.)

At the little school for the Alsatian refugees, of which M. Fernand Gougeon was the head, there was quite a different reaction. The children started screaming as soon as they saw the soldiers and could only be made to leave with difficulty. One of them, Roger Godfrin, aged eight, was the sole survivor of all the schoolchildren. He said later, 'I am from Lorraine and I knew what the Germans could do. I called to my sisters to run away with me but they only cried and wanted to find our mother. I decided to make a break for it and ran into the yard and through the hedge where I lost a shoe. A German fired at me so I dropped down and pretended to be dead. Someone came up and gave me a kick in the back but I didn't move.

'As soon as all seemed quiet I got up and ran as fast as I could. Later I saw two Germans shoot Monsieur Poutaraud near a fence. One of them saw me and fired but he missed. Outside the village some Germans in a small tank chased me but I jumped into a brook and hid under the bank. Later I went into the woods.'

Roger arrived the following day at Laplaud. He was shivering with cold and fright. All the other members of his family perished.*

At 2.45 pm the round-up was almost complete. Tension and fear were mounting among the hundreds of people assembled on the village green, surrounded by the armed soldiers. Some of them clutched their identity papers. Others had not been given time to collect theirs and

* There are six Godfrins on the list of the dead—a man of 37, a woman of 35 and children aged 3, 4, 11 and 13.

were afraid of the consequences. Some mothers carried babies in their arms. Others pushed prams. Many babies, woken from their siesta, were fretful and sniffling. Many women were crying and their husbands were trying to reassure them.

Dr Jacques Desourteaux, the Mayor's son, arriving back in the village after completing his round of patients in the neighbourhood, was compelled to leave his car and join the rest.

The Mayor, in conversation with a German officer through an SS interpreter, was ordered to select a certain number of hostages. He said he couldn't do it and was taken away from the scene to the *mairie* (town hall) where further pressure was put on him. When he returned, a few minutes later, with his escort he was heard to say he would offer himself as a hostage and if others were really necessary they could take his four sons as well.*

At about three o'clock orders were given for the men to be separated from the women and children. This was carried out with shoving and shouting by the SS. Women clung to their husbands and sons and were forcibly separated. As soon as the operation had been completed the women and children were herded out of the square on their way to the church. A few of the mothers had left their babies sleeping in their cots at home and asked, through an interpreter, what they should do. They were told to go and fetch them immediately.

One of the survivors, Monsieur Darthout, said the men were made to sit in three rows facing the houses and forbidden to look round. However he risked a glance and saw the pitiful party leaving the square.

'Many of the women were weeping,' he said. 'Some were on the verge of collapse and had to be supported by the others. I saw my wife for the last time as they turned into the street and disappeared from view. She was in tears.'

The men were addressed by one of the officers. He spoke loudly in German, pausing between sentences for the translation. He said there

* Reports of the number of hostages vary. Most commonly quoted is 30, but one report says five, which may account for the Mayor's offer.

The Laudy barn, two days after the massacre. The five survivors escaped through the hole in the door at the rear.

were secret stores of arms and ammunition for 'terrorists' in the village and they would be found. Anyone who knew of the existence of any weapons of any kind was advised to speak up immediately. A Monsieur Lamaud said he had a 6 mm carbine but explained that this was permitted by the police.

The men were then told that in order to facilitate the search they would be divided into groups and detained in selected buildings. A baker asked if he might return to his shop briefly as he had some pastry in the oven. He was told, 'Don't worry. We'll take care of it.' (An eight-week-old child was later found in the firebox of the oven.)

They were pushed and shoved into groups of between 30 and 70 and marched off to the six buildings. The nearest was the Beaulieu smithy at the entrance to the square. Here, as at the other places, the men concerned were made to carry out certain encumbrances into the street to allow more room inside. The other buildings were barns and garages on or just off the main street. (See map.)

Of the 190 men thus distributed only six got out alive. They were all in the same place, the Laudy barn in the Rue du Cimetière. Their story reveals what must have happened in the other places.

Yvon Roby, an 18-years-old postman, said the party numbered 62 and when they arrived at the barn they were compelled to remove two farm carts before they went inside. They were faced by four young soldiers who chatted and laughed while they fingered their machine guns. One distributed sugar lumps to the others.

Yet, even at this stage, the men could not believe that they were going to be shot. They knew there were no hidden arms in the village and they expected to be released as soon as the search was over. But some of the young ones, like Roby, feared deportation.

Oradour at that moment held its breath. The women and children crammed in the tiny church listened apprehensively. The men facing the firing squads listened for any sound which might convey more comforting thoughts.

At 3.30 a bell sounded in the church tower. It was immediately followed by a burst of machine-gun fire in the main street. It was a signal. The executioners opened fire.

Roby dropped to the ground the instant he realized what was happening. He lay on his stomach protecting his head with his arms. Bullets ricocheted from the wall behind him and he was almost choked with dust. Men had fallen all around him. Some seemed to have been killed instantly but many more were wounded and were moaning and crying.

The fusillade stopped. Spasmodic revolver shots followed, punctuated by groans. Roby realized the SS were finishing off anyone who seemed to be still alive.

'I waited, petrified, for the bullet that would kill me,' he said, 'but they must have thought I was dead. My left arm was numb. I had been wounded in the elbow. All about me the moaning was stopping. There were fewer shots. Eventually all was quiet.'

The soldiers piled faggots, straw, hurdles, ladders and anything else they could find that was combustible on top of the bodies. Then they withdrew. Roby heard what seemed to be a radio playing in the street. There was a German voice followed by music.

Then he realized he was not the only one left alive. Faint cries issued from the pile of bodies. He slowly turned his head and saw one of his friends lying on his side covered in blood. He was still breathing.

The soldiers returned and set fire to the straw. The flames spread rapidly and Roby knew he was in danger of being burned alive.

'I tried to move,' he said, 'but the weight of the bodies made it difficult and, because of my wound, I couldn't use my left arm. However, after a desperate struggle I got free and stood up. I expected to be shot. But the brutes had left the barn.'

The flames drove him against the wall and he could hardly breathe. Then he saw that one of the panels of a door at the back of the barn had been broken open and he squeezed through. He found himself in another barn and, to his surprise, realized he had been preceded by four others. They were Messieurs Broussaudier, Darthout, Borie and Hébras. A sixth, Monsieur Poutaraud, had got out another way. (Roger Godfrin saw him shot.)

Three of them hid behind some faggots. Roby sought cover under a pile of straw and beans. Darthout had been hit four times in the legs and was bleeding profusely. He begged Roby to find a place for him. Roby dragged him under his cover.

'We clung together like brothers,' he said.

They lay there, hardly daring to move, while they listened, terror-stricken, to the noises outside.

Suddenly a soldier entered the barn. They held their breaths. A lighter clicked and they realized he had set fire to the straw. The flames were soon scorching Roby's feet. In a desperate movement he raised his head. The soldier had gone. Broussaudier found another exit and the others followed him, pursued by the flames.

They sought shelter in a rabbit house where Roby, using his right arm and his feet, managed to excavate a hole big enough to hold his body and pulled surrounding material over it to conceal himself. The others also hid, helping the wounded Darthout.

Roby reckoned they must have stayed there about three hours listening to the frightful sounds outside. An appalling outburst of screaming came from somewhere lower down the village. Later the roar and crackle of a big fire became louder and nearer.

Eventually their shelter caught fire and cinders fell from the roof on to Roby's head. It was obvious they would have to move again and quickly.

They emerged from the rabbit house into a cloud of smoke which fortunately concealed their movements. They slowly made their way to the Champ de Foire by a back street. Then came the danger of crossing the village green. Although the houses all around were on fire and smoke swept over the whole scene, they were terrified of being spotted.

Broussaudier decided to risk a sprint across the green to the cemetery. There was no shot. The others followed as quickly as they could, carrying the crippled Darthout. At the cemetery they crawled into thick undergrowth where they felt they were safe at last.

'We embraced each other fervently,' said Roby, 'so intense was our relief.'

Roby, who lived in the hamlet of La Basse-Forêt, spent the night in a field of barley and arrived home the following morning at about 11 o'clock.

Darthout, describing his escape, said he was hit in the calves during the first fusillade and suffered additional wounds in his thighs. This confirms the theory that the SS deliberately fired low to cripple their victims so that they would be burned alive. But if one believes Roby's account why then did they climb over the wounded men finishing off anyone who seemed to be alive?

Darthout was covered with blood from the men who fell on him. When the firing stopped he tentatively moved his hand and felt it grasped by another. It was Aliotti who whispered that both his legs were also broken.

Some of those who escaped:
Back row *(left to right):* Roby, Darthout, Beaubreuil Jr, Desourteaux, Renaud. Front row: Armand Senon, Borie, Daniel Senon, Broussaudier, Roger Godfrin, Beaubrevil Sr, Besson, Doutre, Machefer.

One of the wounded lifted his head and whispered that the soldiers had gone. They could be heard in the street. Darthout also heard music.* Aliotti called the names of his wife and children and bid his friends goodbye.

When the soldiers lit the pyre Darthout's hair caught fire and he beat it out with his hands. While he struggled to free himself he was badly burned in the shoulder. As he crawled away from the flames he realized from the cries around him that many of his friends were being burned alive. But, in his crippled state, he could do nothing to help them. He found himself being helped by three others who had managed to make a

---

* This playing of music during a massacre seems to have been a peculiarity of the SS. At Ascq in northern France where 86 men were executed following the derailment of a troop train, the soldiers played gramophone records while they carried out the butchery. They did the same thing at Tulle while 99 men were being hanged.

The Church before and after the massacre.

hole in the door at the rear.

Robert Hébras said they were shut in the barn for a while after they had removed the farm carts. When the soldiers opened the door again they hoped they were going to be liberated. However, they were ordered to clear a patch of the floor near the entrance. The soldiers brought in two machine guns and ordered the men to line up in rows facing them.

'I think we knew then that it was all over,' he said. Some of the men held hands, some folded their arms. One or two turned their backs to the guns. The machine guns were fired in two long bursts. He thought most of the men were hit in the chest.

Exactly what happened at the other places of execution no one, apart

from the killers, lived to describe. But when the salvage teams eventually penetrated the ruins they found the remains of some women and children among those of the men in a barn on the green facing the church. Women's remains were also found in another barn.

The women locked in the church with the children suffered much physical discomfort, apart from agony of mind. It is estimated that there were over 200 of them with about the same number of children crammed into an edifice intended for a congregation of not more than 350.

The schoolchildren crowded round their teachers, except where they

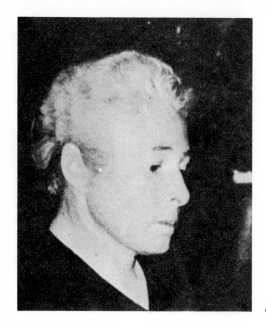
Madame Rouffanche.

were taken in hand by their parents. Many had come from hamlets and houses outside the village and their parents were expecting their return that afternoon.

Little Dominique Forest had been separated from his brother but he did have his aunt, Madame Rousseau, to comfort him.

A Limoges journalist, Pierre Poitevin,* (author of *Dans l'Enfer d'Oradour*) who visited Madame Rouffanche in hospital and was one of

* Poitevin took photographs, surreptitiously, of the ruins, the remains of the dead and the salvage teams at work. He was arrested by some German soldiers, placed against a wall, and feared he would be shot. However, he managed to persuade his captors that he was an insurance agent attending to the interests of the relatives of the victims. Fortunately they didn't notice the bulge of his folding camera in his trousers pocket; his bicycle was taken by the Germans but later returned to him.

the first to enter the ruins says the infants in their prams and pushchairs were placed in one of the side chapels (the Chapel of St Anne). The women prayed aloud for their menfolk.

Suddenly the sound of gunfire was heard. For a moment they looked at each other in horror. Then they began to weep, but tried to contain their grief when the children crowded round them asking what was the matter. Then a key grated in the lock of the main door.

Marguerite Rouffanche, who was 47, had been rounded up with her family and kept with them. She said the door burst open and two young soldiers carried in a heavy case from which 'long white cords' trailed. They deposited the case near the altar, lit the cords and hastily retreated, locking the door again.

The women backed away from the sinister 'case'. Children were trampled on, chairs overturned. Suddenly there was an explosion, and black, suffocating smoke poured from the case.*

Everyone crowded in panic into the side chapels and pressed up to the doors and windows. They coughed, choked and screamed as they inhaled the smoke.

'The door of the vestry was burst open by the force of one panic-stricken group,' said Madame Rouffanche. 'I went through with them and sat on one of the steps. My daughter came to join me. Then the Germans noticed that the vestry had been entered and fired at us through the windows. My daughter was killed by my side. I owe my life to the fact that I shut my eyes and played dead.'

She heard shooting and screaming in the body of the church and the detonation of grenades. The SS had burst in through the main entrance and were firing into the seething, screaming mass, finishing the job the smoke grenades had failed to do.

When the screaming died down, Madame Rouffanche heard the soldiers gathering together chairs and other combustible material to pile on the bodies. She heard them leave when they had set fire to the pyre.

* The case was packed with glass grenades of the type used by the Germans to winkle out tank crews. It seems to have been specially prepared for asphyxiating the people in the church.

As the flames mounted it became evident that many of the women had, like Madame Rouffanche, been feigning death. They screamed again as the flames reached them. Many were badly wounded and could not move.

'I got to my feet,' said Madame Rouffanche, 'and, concealed by the smoke, slipped behind the altar where there are three windows. I got hold of the step ladder which they used for lighting the tall candles and managed to reach the centre window, the largest. I still don't know how I managed it but I squeezed through that window and dropped three metres to the ground.'

Then she realized from a sound above that she was being followed. A young mother—Madame Henriette Joyeux, aged 23—was holding out her seven-months-old baby and pleading with Madame Rouffanche to catch it. She tried, but couldn't manage to hold it and the child hit the ground.

The infant's screams probably attracted the attention of some soldiers in the street below for as the two women hurried in the direction of the presbytery garden they were fired on. Marguerite Rouffanche was hit five times, four times in the legs. The fifth bullet shattered a shoulder blade. However, she managed to drag herself into the garden where she hid among some rows of peas and tried to cover herself with earth.

Henriette Joyeux and her baby were mortally wounded. The baby's skull had been shattered. She managed to get as far as the privy in the garden where she died. Her body, with the baby's, was subsequently found in a trench dug by a number of soldiers who returned to the scene on Monday morning.

The rest of the dreadful story could only be pieced together from evidence found by the salvage teams. Again it appeared that in many cases the executioners had fired low to cripple their victims when they realized that the asphyxiation plan wasn't going to work. Bodies which had not been consumed by the flames had shattered legs. From the attitudes and location of many of the corpses it was evident that they had been burned alive.

Many children must have been killed outright by the firing and the

The window (lower centre) through which Madame Rouffanche escaped.

The same window seen from inside the church. Note the remains of a pram in the foreground.

The wooden confessional in which the two little boys were found shot in the back of the neck.

grenades. Babies' bodies were found in the remains of prams. In the right transept a huge pile of charred human remains was found in front of a little door which was locked. Yet it appeared that this door had been open at first and two women and eight children had got out that way. Their bodies were found in the cellar of the presbytery.

The wooden confessional in the left transept, which was surprisingly unaffected by the fire, contained the bodies of two little boys who had been shot in the back of the neck. One report said that the body of a child in an attitude of prayer was found before the altar.

There were many isolated killings in and around the village. Bedridden veterans were shot where they lay or allowed to burn to death in their homes. The body of a man was found lightly interred in his garden with one hand sticking above ground. Other bodies were found in a well and in the oven of a bakery.

An unlucky party of young people—five boys and a girl—were seen to arrive at the Champ de Foire, pushing their bicycles, just after the round-up. They were subsequently lined up against the wall of the Beaulieu Forge, in which a group of men was shot, and mown down with a machine gun.

Jules Renaudin who, with his wife, was employed by the Vicomtesse de Saint-Venant at Laplaud Manor insisted on going into the village after the shooting had started. He was warned of the danger and went to his death saying he must get his tobacco ration and would pick up his eleven-years-old daughter Bernadette who was a pupil at the Lorraine school.

There were some miraculous escapes. A carpenter named Beaubreuil hid his two sons under the floor of his living room when he saw the SS arrive. He feared they would be deported. They lay there until the house started to burn. They escaped through the backyard and didn't stop running until they got to St Victurnien, eight kms away.

Another young man, Paul Doutre, managed to escape being rounded up although he saw his parents being hustled to the Champ de Foire as he peered through the shutters.

When the house was set alight he crept out of the garage where he was hiding and tried to rescue some personal belongings from his room. He was spotted and driven back into the garage at gunpoint. He managed to get through a window into the garden. When the roof of the garage fell in he heard the soldiers who had mounted guard in front remark 'Kaput!' and move on, laughing.

One of the Mayor's sons, Hubert Desourteaux, aged 29, was another survivor. He owned a garage in the village. He was particularly perturbed when the SS arrived because he was an escaped prisoner-of-war. He managed to hide at home when the round-up took place and heard the fusillades, not realizing that a group of men were being shot in his garage. While his house was burning he ran into the yard and hid among some hazel bushes. He later moved to an outbuilding.

His mechanic, Aimé Renaud, also escaped. His wife, Jeanine, ran to

33

the garage to warn him that the SS were coming and they hid in their employer's yard while he was in the house. They stayed there, concealed by a pile of stones and some bushes, listening to the appalling sounds in the village. They did not dare emerge from their hiding place until after midnight when Madame Renaud almost collided with a soldier. Fortunately he didn't see her. They feared for the safety of their four-year-old daughter Annie (who died in the church) and Madame Renaud's mother, who was also dead at that time. Together they managed to get out of the ruined village and across the river to try to find Monsieur Renaud's parents.

Hippolyte Senon, a young man, had cycled out of Oradour just before the place was surrounded. He went to several farms and hamlets warning people not to go to Oradour. One of the places he visited was a mill on the Glane, where the miller's young wife, Solange, was terrified for the safety of her husband. He had insisted on going to Oradour on his bicycle, waving a white handkerchief as he entered. She joined other women, including mothers of children at school in the village, to watch with mounting horror and fear the appalling sight of the buildings catching fire one after the other.

A tenant farmer named Gaudy left one of the cottages near the Laplaud Manor to go and find his three children who were at school. He was pulled up short on the road by the terrible screams from the church.

One frantic mother, fearful about the fate of her four children, actually succeeded in getting in and out of the village during the SS occupation. She was Madame Démery whose children, André (13), Henri (12), Ernest (11) and Marcelle (10), had been taken to the church when she arrived. Accompanied by a neighbour, she reached the children's school through the smoke of burning houses. They heard screaming and shooting at the lower end of the village but saw no soldiers. Frantic with fear, they burst into the school. Madame Démery saw her boys' caps and satchels but the place was empty.

Another parent who got in and out during the occupation was a Monsieur Déschamps, a farm worker of La Fauvette. He thought the woods near Oradour were on fire and as his four daughters had not returned from school he decided to go to the village to see what was happening. He entered Oradour at the top end which was sparsely guarded and was surprised to find that the main street was deserted. The doors of the houses were open but not a soul was in sight. He entered the boys' school, near the tram station, and found it deserted. He was on his way down to the girls' school when he saw armed soldiers and decided to return home. He told his wife he thought the whole population had been evacuated. The bodies of their daughters—Claudine (13), Renee (11), Huguette (8) and Maryse (6)—were among those which were never identified.

At the Laplaud Manor Madame Forest became alarmed when she heard the noise of the shooting and screams which carried a long way. Why had not Michel returned with little Dominique? If there had been any danger they would have come back, bringing her father with them. Accompanied by Dr and Madame Gaudois, who were also staying at the Manor, she walked down the drive to the edge of the woods where they had a view of Oradour. They also thought there was a forest fire on the other side of the village. 'If there is any danger to the village,' they assured each other, 'the people will have been evacuated.'

There were two incidents connected with the tramway. During the afternoon a test tram from Limoges bearing company employees arrived at the outskirts of the village. One of the passengers, a Monsieur Chalard, got down to find out what was happening. He was shot as he crossed the bridge over the Glane and his body was thrown into the river. The tram returned to Limoges.

Towards seven o'clock, when the fire was at its height, a second tram full of passengers arrived. One can imagine their feelings as the vehicle slowly approached the burning village. One of the guards at the bridge ordered the driver to stop. No one was allowed to descend, while a soldier went off on a bicycle to get orders. He returned in about five minutes with the instructions that everyone bound for Oradour was to get out, while the rest were to return to Limoges.

The luckless passengers, numbering 22, were marched off at gunpoint almost as far as the hamlet of Les Bordes. They crossed the Glane by a footbridge which was basically a tree trunk. They were halted near a house which had been taken over as a command post.

An NCO conferred with an officer. Then the men were separated from the women and papers were checked. The two parties were reunited. There was further discussion between the soldiers.

One of the passengers, Mademoiselle Louise Compain, who was anxious about her parents in Oradour, said some of them asked the soldiers what had happened to the villagers. *'Tous kaput!'* they were told.

'We thought there may have been a fight between the Maquis and the Germans but one of them told us in halting French, "We found arms and ammunition there. So we blew everything up and burnt the place."'

Mademoiselle Compain said most of the soldiers were laughing and chattering as if they had enjoyed what they had been doing. However, she noticed one young one sitting on a stone and apparently weeping. He kept wiping his eyes with the sleeve of his uniform.

Suddenly, as if they had reached a decision, the captors encircled their victims and pointed their guns at them. The petrified people were convinced that this was the preliminary to their execution. There was further conversation between the officer and the NCO. Then, to their immense relief, they were told they were free to go.

An interpreter told them, 'You can consider yourselves lucky!' And they didn't know until later just how lucky they were. As they prepared to hurry away from the burning village—which they were barred from entering—one of the soldiers offered a girl a bicycle he had stolen.

The survivors from the village included a Monsieur Crémoux, a repatriated prisoner-of-war who managed to get out just before the place was surrounded. For a while he hid in the bushes by the river. He was actually in the water, with his head sticking out in the shadow of the bank when two soldiers passed by. He heard one say to the other, 'I killed 26 of them'.

Monsieur Armand Senon, whose home overlooked the Champ de

The tramlines running along the Rue Emile Desourteaux.

Foire, stayed in his room during the round-up. He had a broken leg in a plaster cast sustained in a game of football. When he heard the fusillades, after the men had been marched away, he realized that flight was imperative. He limped out of his back door and hid in his garden.

Peering through the undergrowth he saw soldiers firing at people who had escaped the round-up. In fact, they seemed to be firing at everything that moved, including cats, dogs and hens.

'One of the bastards, a red-headed fellow, crouched down within a few feet of where I was hiding to relieve himself,' he said. 'For one mad moment I thought of braining him with my walking stick.'

A neighbour, Monsieur Machefer, also escaped but his wife failed to follow him and was taken to the church.

One entire family, together with a woman friend, had an amazing escape. They decided to stay indoors when the order for assembly was given. A soldier burst in and shoved the two women and two children into the street, ordering them to go to the Champ de Foire. The father, hidden in a bedroom, thought he had been overlooked but another soldier found him and he was made to join the rest of the family outside. However, for some reason or other their escort was momentarily distracted and they all managed to slip away and hide in the undergrowth at the back of the houses. Later they got away into the woods.

At about 7 o'clock, when the firing had died down, Professor Forest, frantic with worry about his two sons, approached the guard at the lower end of the village. He started to talk in German, then lapsed into French which the SS man understood. He was an Alsatian. As they stood, 25 yards from the burning church where the remains of the women and children were settling into a charred mass, the soldier said all the women and children had gone into the woods and were safe. The professor returned to Laplaud. That night, while the other Forest children slept, their parents sat on Dominique's empty bed sleepless and worried.

At Orbagnac, Madame Catherine Lévêque was also frightened. Her daughter Yvonne had gone to Oradour during the afternoon to get some yeast for her mother. Yvonne had been accompanied by a friend,

Marcelle Ratier. Neither had returned.

At 3 am Madame Lévêque suddenly screamed, 'We'll never have our child back! I see a pile of charred bones!' Her husband decided to go into Oradour while it was still dark. He circled the village and eventually got inside. He got a terrible impression of death everywhere and returned without hope of ever seeing his daughter alive again.

At 5 am Professor Forest went back to Oradour. He asked a sentry in German, 'Where are the children?'. This time he got the blunt reply 'They are all dead' and he was shoved off at gunpoint. As he walked dejectedly up the drive at Laplaud he heard his wife screaming. Later they received the news of the escape of Aimé and Jeanine Renaud who were their cousins. They hurried to the house at La Plaine whence, they were told, the Renauds had gone. But they received no comforting news there. So Professor Forest returned to the village for the third time. As he crossed the river bridge the smoke and stench blowing his way brought tears to his eyes. This time he persuaded the guard to take him to an officer who shouted that he knew nothing about the children and advised him to get out of the place or he'd be treated like a terrorist.

Houses outside a certain radius were spared. At one of these a certain Madame Sage was watching the burning of Oradour when she was suddenly visited by five soldiers. They forced her at gunpoint to make omelettes for them and provide wine. They told her that the village was destroyed because there were terrorists there who had killed an important SS officer.

The first parent to get into the ruined church was a farmer named Hyvernaud. His two sons, Marcel (12) and André (6), had not returned and at 4.30 am he decided to investigate. As if by instinct, he went straight to the church.

Among the blackened, stinking human remains he recognized the half-burnt body of André. His throat had been severed and one leg was broken and twisted back. He still wore one of his sabots.

Monsieur Hyvernaud returned to his farm at Le Breuil, two kms north-east of Oradour, and told his wife. They returned to the church with some sheets. They couldn't recognize Marcel among the other remains so they wrapped up what was left of André and took him home. They buried him in the farmyard.

During his search for his other son Monsieur Hyvernaud had passed behind the altar where he found the remains of about 20 small children who appeared to have been put there in the hope that they would be safe. He saw a number of dead babies in their bullet-riddled prams.

All the houses had been looted and valuables—radios, drink and food—were loaded into the lorries. As each house was cleared, the interior was doused with petrol and ignited. Grenades were used to spread the flames.

However, one building, La Maison Dupic, a draper's shop, was not destroyed with the rest. It was emptied of much of its stock but the SS had a use for it later. It was selected as a sort of guard post for the night. The rearguard had an orgy there with much drinking and singing. They set fire to the place when they left at about 11 am. About 25 empty champagne bottles were subsequently found in the ruins.

Monsieur Armand Senon, the survivor with the broken leg, heard the last of the lorries leave but dared not leave his hiding place in the woods until several hours later.

When he cautiously made his way into the ruins he almost immediately came upon the body of Monsieur Poutaraud, the garage proprietor who had survived the shooting in the Laudy barn. He had been shot in the back and his body was half way through a fence. A live horse was tethered to one of his dead arms. It was cropping the grass.

The first living soul he met was Monsieur Desvignes, the butcher, who told him that everyone had been killed and their bodies burned. He was in tears. Monsieur Senon searched in vain for any trace of his family.

A few other people made a cautious appearance, staring in horror at the ruins. The transformation of a peaceful, picturesque place into a smoking, stinking ruin was shocking in itself without investigation of what the ruins contained. Certain landmarks were recognizable because their signs were still legible, if somewhat charred—Hôtel Milord, Hôtel Beaubreuil, Restaurant Dagoury, Café du Chêne, Boulangerie,

Boucherie, etc. But they bore no resemblance to the busy, places of the previous day.

Horses and cattle roamed the streets looking for their sta barns. Dogs sniffed among the ruins for their masters, whi shivering. All the cats had taken refuge in a house on the outskirts which had been spared and were howling to be fed. Swallows darted about distraught because their nests had gone. Poultry and rabbits foraged in the gardens.

In all, 254 buildings were destroyed including 123 houses. When the list of the dead came to be drawn up it was established that the residents, together with the refugees, totalled 393. People who had come in from the countryside totalled 167. There were 33 people from Limoges and 43 from other places. Six others were subsequently added to the list when it turned out that they had disappeared and must have been in Oradour at the time.

One man whose name was not listed was Obersturmführer Knug of the SS. He was killed by a stone from the church steeple when it collapsed. His family was told that he had been killed in action, fighting for the Führer and Fatherland.

Among the others who entered the village later on Sunday were Hubert Desourteaux and Monsieur Lévignac, who still hoped to find his sons, Serge and Charles. Lévignac went into the church and soon emerged shocked and unbelieving. Then he heard a faint cry of pain and traced the source to the presbytery garden where he found what he thought was a negress lying along the rows of peas. It was Marguerite Rouffanche, who had covered herself with earth. She was so distraught that she begged her rescuers to throw her into the river. She had been lying there for nearly 24 hours. They put her in a wheelbarrow and took her to Laplaud. She was covered with a mixture of blood and soil. She could hardly speak but her rescuers could just distinguish a repeated phrase, 'All the women and children were burned in the church.'

At the Manor Dr Gaudois cut away her clothing and did the best he could to clean her up. He realized that her five bullet wounds needed urgent attention but he had no facilities. However, they kept her at the

.Manor overnight and smuggled her into Limoges hospital the next day with false identity papers. Once, to their horror, the rescuers were stopped by a sentry but they managed to convince him that their patient had fallen from a hay loft.

Pierre Poitevin visited Marguerite Rouffanche in hospital a few days after the tragedy with a friend of hers. She had refused to see anyone (particularly journalists) except a few friends and relatives. Poitevin did not reveal his identity and she did not query it.

She spoke in a low voice about the terrible scenes in the church. She said her two daughters, Andrée Rouffanche, aged 21, and Madame Amélie Péyroux (23), had gone into the vestry with her. In the rush Amélie had dropped her baby. She had found him shortly before they were both killed by bullets.

Madame Rouffanche said she was so sorry she had been unable to catch Henriette Joyeux's baby when she dropped it from the window.

She told how she tried to cover herself with earth while she lay among the peas. Her wounds were very painful and she suffered greatly from thirst. She managed to clutch a few handfuls of peas and chewed them to alleviate her thirst.

Early on Sunday morning she heard men's voices. She slowly turned her head and saw some soldiers milking a cow a short distance away. When they moved away she tried to crawl further into the undergrowth but her wounds made it impossible. Then she wanted to crawl down to the Glane and die there. But she couldn't move.

After the sacking of Oradour the SS travelled to the village of Nieul, about six miles away, where billets had been arranged for the night. Someone who saw them pass en route said some of them were singing to an accordion. Residents of Nieul described how they arrived in a state of excitement. They spread out in the streets shouting to each other. Some appeared to be drunk. Most of the soldiers were billeted in the village school. After washing off their grime in the children's toilets they drank their looted liquor and settled down for the night in the classrooms. The officers spent the night together in one room of a private house.

The following day, Sunday, 11 June, the soldiers cooked and ate the poultry they had stolen. Some of them fooled around in the playground with two new bicycles until they smashed them. These were identified as having been taken from Oradour, as also was a motor-cycle found in a park pond.

One soldier was seen at the ground floor window of a house distributing banknotes from two canteens.

Two French lorry drivers, Messieurs Démery and Nadaud, who were commissioned to help with the transport of the battalion's accoutrements from St Junien, said an Alsatian told them, 'We have just carried out quite a job. We have killed all the people of Oradour and burned them in the church.'

The last of the soldiers to leave Oradour on Sunday morning, after the burning of the Maison Dupic, were seen en route to Nieul by Hubert Desourteaux. Their trucks were loaded with loot and they were towing a car which he recognized as belonging to one of his customers. In the centre of La Plaine the rope broke and the car crashed into one of the poles which carried the electric wires for the tramway. The man at the wheel was badly hurt. The others put him in a truck, together with the loot from the car, set fire to the car and carried on.

The soldiers in Nieul spent much of Sunday in a state of readiness seated in the lorries. They were joined by other companies of the battalion and a party was despatched to burn the Château de Morcheval in the neighbourhood.

On the morning of Monday the 12th a party of SS returned to Oradour. Their orders were apparently to try to conceal some of the evidence of the atrocities. They dug two trenches in which they deposited half-consumed bodies. One trench was near the church, the other near the Denys Garage where a group of men had been shot. They also buried a number of isolated corpses on the outskirts. Before leaving they fired bursts on their machine guns. They were seen to leave in the direction of Limoges.

For a few days the Germans put a guard on the ruins and forbade entry to anyone except an official salvage team. Some SS officers paid an unexpected visit, apparently to make a report. They left with some stray poultry.

The first official salvage team consisted mainly of Red Cross workers assisted by young seminarists. They worked with rubber gloves and had handkerchiefs soaked in eucalyptus tied over their noses and mouths. The stench had become almost unbearable.

Identification of some of the half-burnt bodies was possible but the vast majority of the people were never identified. In fact out of the 642 dead only 52 could be named. The others were just a mass of charred flesh and bone.

The most heart-rending task was the clearing of the church. A man who was a member of the rescue team suddenly recognized the body of his wife who seemed to be clasping her mother. As he moved to touch them the bodies disintegrated. The remains of Denise Bardet were recognized amid what must have been a number of her pupils.

One report said that the body of the parish priest was found in the church but this was never substantiated. There were three priests in the village on that fatal afternoon—the Abbé Chapelle, the parish priest, the Abbé Lorich from Alsace-Lorraine, and the young seminarist, Emile Francois-Xavier Neumeyer. They all disappeared without trace although the first two were seen in the assembly at the Champ de Foire.

Among the remains of the women was found a large number of belt buckles, corset stiffeners, powder compacts and lipstick holders. A letter stained with blood which had somehow escaped being burned was addressed to a priest and dated 10 June. It started, 'I am quite well at present and benefiting from the sunshine . . .'

A page of an exercise book belonging to an 11-year-old pupil bore the sentence copied from the blackboard, *'Je prends la resolution de ne jamais faire de mal aux autres.'*

It was surprising that the crucifix against the exterior wall of the church, near the main entrance, which had recently been resilvered, was unscathed, as also was a wooden crucifix fixed to the wall of a burnt house.

Above: *Burial party, wearing handkerchiefs soaked in eucalyptus, recovering charred remains from one of the execution sites.*
Below: *Passing through the Champ de Foire on the way to the cemetery. (These pictures were taken surreptitiously by Pierre Poitevin, a journalist from Limoges, two days after the massacre.)*

The tabernacle had been forced open and the sacred vessels stolen. This act was mentioned in a despatch from Monseigneur Rastouil, Bishop of Limoges, to General Gleiniger, commander of the German garrison in the city.

The Bishop wrote 'You will appreciate my indignation when I heard that the church of Oradour-sur-Glane had been violated by the execution within its walls of hundreds of women and children and profaned by the theft of the sacred pyx. . . . It is my duty to find out what happened to the sacred vessels, not so much for their value as for what they contained—the consecrated host.'

Gleiniger, a Wehrmacht officer, was probably unaware of the massacre at the time it was committed, not being in the confidence of the SS. He expressed his regrets to the Bishop and said he was shocked when he heard the news. One report said that he told one of his officers, 'It would have been better for Germany to lose another five divisions than to carry the guilt of the massacre of Oradour.'

Salvage work on any scale could not be started until 14 June. Dr Bapt, the medical officer of health for the area, compiled a report. He said the bodies which could be identified were buried separately, each with its individual cross. The majority of the human remains were interred in two communal graves. Personal objects of value found with the bodies or in the ruins were deposited in a bank together with identity papers.

Dead animals also had to be buried or burned. In the ruins of one farm were the remains of 30 sheep.

Dr Bapt reported that on 19 June he had gone to Les Bordes on his bicycle when he was told that the Germans had returned to Oradour. He hurried back and found three lorry-loads of soldiers at the southern entrance to the ruins. Some were in the village and he saw two of them removing the wheels of two cars. Dr Bapt presented his permit and found his salvage team still at work. They told him that the Germans had at first seized their bicycles and loaded them into the lorries. However, they got them back when they convinced the Germans of their identity and their task.

The Gestapo soon got to hear that there were survivors and did their utmost to trace them. Fortunately they were warned by the *Maquis* and helped to find shelter. The injured ones were treated surreptitiously. The Resistance also helped the survivors financially as no official monetary help was given until mid-July.

The SS left the region on 12 June heading for the Normandy battlefield. On 13 June the Bishop of Limoges visited the ruins. On 16 June he told the story of what had happened to a huge congregation in Limoges cathedral. He announced that a memorial service would be held on 21 June at 9.30 am.

The Gestapo and the Militia (French collaborationist troops) got to hear about the service and planned to stop it. They spread a rumour that the cathedral had been mined. But the people ignored it. A large proportion of them knew Oradour well and had spent happy times there. They flocked to the cathedral and the congregation overflowed into the street. The whole city went into mourning. Shops and cafés were closed and work stopped.

On Monday, 19 June, the German censor in Limoges, Doctor Sahm, called a meeting of local journalists. He told them Oradour had been full of *Maquis*. In fact, on 9 June and even on the morning of the 10th German vehicles had been fired on. The action of the SS could therefore be described as a defensive one. However, he added, it was not clear what had happened in the church. It was possible that the officers of the unit concerned would be court-martialled.

Then, after a pause, 'But, of course, gentlemen, you will appreciate that many more women and children have been killed by RAF bombers than at Oradour.'

He ordered Press silence on the matter. However, death notices for the victims appeared in the local papers in ever-increasing numbers until they were forbidden.

On 22 June, Monseigneur Valerio Valeri, the Papal Nuncio at Vichy, sent a note of protest to Pétain. He expressed horror at what had happened at Oradour and implored the Marshal to transmit the feelings of the people to the German High Command. Pétain wrote to Hitler complaining about the campaign of reprisals which, he said 'would gravely compromise the reconciliation of our two peoples'. There was no reply.

Eventually the Militia arrested the Bishop of Limoges and held him under open arrest at Châteauroux from which he was liberated after intervention by the Papal Nuncio.

The attitude of the Vichy Government was expressed by a spokesman, Xavier Vallat, in a broadcast on the controlled radio on 27 June. He was referring to a woman who had died at Oradour.

'The French people are morally responsible for the death of this woman and many others,' he said, and went on to explain that if they had not provoked the occupation of the southern part of France and allowed a group of 'bandits' to cause grave unrest in the name of false patriotism the Germans would not have been obliged to inflict punishment on so many innocent people.

③ The Guilty

The massacre at Oradour-sur-Glane was carried out by a detachment of the third company of the 1st Battalion of No. 4 Panzergrenadier Regiment ('*Der Führer*') of the Das Reich Division of the Waffen SS. The operation was led by the Battalion commander, Sturmbannführer Otto Dickmann, assisted by Hauptsturmführer Kahn, C.O. of the third company.*

This is the full list of the people directly or indirectly involved in the massacre and what became of them:

The German High Command, who, basically were responsible for all German war crimes.

General Fritz Von Brodowski, commander of the Clermont-Ferrand Region. Shot on 28 October, 1944 while trying to escape from the Citadel at Besançon where he awaited trial for war crimes.

General Heinz Bernard Lammerding, C.O. of the Das Reich Division of the Waffen SS. Wounded in Normandy on 25 July, 1944 by shell splinters. After hospital treatment he resumed command of the division in mid-October until January, 1945. Eight days before the German surrender he was hospitalized again and abandoned his uniform. He was captured by the Americans but soon escaped. He reappeared at Dusseldorf in July, 1945 and obtained an identity card from the British occupying authority. He resumed his former profession of civil engineer. The British refused to extradite him for the Oradour trial in 1953. He died in Bavaria on 13 January, 1971 of lung cancer.

* For equivalent British Army ranks see page 87.

Obersturmbannführer Sylvester Stadler, C.O. of the *Der Führer* Regt. Promoted to command the Hohenstaufen Division of the Waffen SS on 28 June 1944; wounded in late July in Normandy. He got back to Germany and was known to be alive at the time of the Oradour trial. Subsequent history not known.

Sturmbannführer Otto Dickmann, C.O. of the 1st Battalion of the *Der Führer* Regt. Killed in the fighting around Falaise in August, 1944.

Hauptsturmführer Kahn, C.O. of the third company. Wounded in the arm and lost an eye in the Normandy battlefield. Got back to Germany where he and his wife 'disappeared' with their family. In 1953 he was reported to be in Sweden.

Oberscharführer Joachim Kleist, of the Limoges Gestapo. Fate unknown.

There is one man whose name is not included in this list and yet it was his impatience that was the spur for the Oradour massacre, as will be seen. But first it is important to explore the origins of the Das Reich Division.

The SS or Schutzstaffel (Protection Squad) was founded as a personal guard for Hitler. In 1929 when he appointed Heinrich Himmler, aged 28, as Reichsführer SS, there were about 280 men in it. Himmler was instructed to create an elite Nazi troop, utterly dependable in all circumstances. In 1933, when Hitler became Chancellor, the SS had swelled to 52,000.

They were still nominally part of the SA (Stürmabteilung) or Brown-shirts who numbered 300,000. In 1934 this organization, led by Ernst Röhm, was getting out of hand and demanding a revolution. Hitler decided to purge it. He wanted to come to terms with the Army. He used his SS for the notorious assassinations of 30 June, 1934, the 'Night of the Long Knives', when Röhm and other SA officers were liquidated.

In the years just prior to the war the combat units of the SS grew in number, not as part of the Army but as a standing armed force at Hitler's personal disposal. Selection of recruits was based on racial and physical standards of a high degree. They were subjected to intensive indoctrination politically and ideologically.

The SS were prominent in the occupation of the Sudetenland, Austria and Czechoslovakia. On the outbreak of war they went into action with the Army and proved to be fearless, relentless fighters. Their strength was soon increased to three divisions. During the war they rose to 38 divisions.

Complaints about atrocities committed by the SS arose early in the war. They came mainly from the Army. But Hitler warned the generals that there would be activities in the conquered territory which 'might not be to their taste'. He also warned them not to interfere.

Fifty Jews who had been rounded up in Poland for forced labour were shot by the SS. The Army commander in the area concerned insisted that the men responsible should be court-martialled. They were given short terms of imprisonment for manslaughter. Himmler subsequently quashed the sentences.

But, despite the lack of trust between the Wehrmacht and the SS, the Army generals had to admit that during the early years of the war the SS were exceptional in discipline and soldierly bearing. In fact they were regarded, and regarded themselves, as an elite military formation.

Ulrich von Hassell has described the SS as having 'an ambiguous psychology'. In them 'two souls lived in strange confusion, one barbarian, the soul of the Nazi party, the other a perverted aristocratic soul.' Their blind ideology led to heavy casualties in their ranks. They were taught to be contemptuous of death, their own as well as their adversaries. They were judged not by the size of their losses but by the glory of their achievements.

When, eventually, some high-ranking Wehrmacht officers were persuaded to take command of the SS, casualties tended to fall while the military achievement remained high. However, these experienced commanders were not always able to control the actions of their less experienced junior officers.

The Das Reich division of the Waffen (Fighting) SS originated in October, 1939. It fought under the title of SS VT Division (Motorized). In December, 1940, its name was changed to SS Division Deutschland, but to avoid confusion with an existing regiment of that name it became known as SS Division Reich in January, 1941.

The Division was to the fore in the invasion of Jugoslavia and accepted the surrender of Belgrade. Its men were ruthless in the suppression of a revolt of the young people there. It subsequently went to Russia where it spearheaded the attack on Moscow. It suffered heavy casualties in the Russian winter counter-offensive.

In March, 1942, the Division returned to Germany to be regrouped and in November it became an armoured division in the SS Panzer Korps, which was sent into the thick of the Russian campaign. It was instrumental in halting the big Russian counter-offensive of that time and in recapturing Kharkov, for which it received a special commendation from Field-Marshal von Manstein. (Hitler told a group of dinner guests: 'I am proud when an Army commander can tell me that his force is based essentially on an armoured division and the SS Reich Division.')

In December, 1943, after suffering very heavy losses, the Division was withdrawn to Germany for reinforcement. An advance staff was sent to Stablack in East Prussia and early in February, 1944, some of the Division was transferred to a new training centre at Bordeaux.

The remainder of the Division continued to fight in Russia for a while as 'Kämpfgruppe Das Reich' (unofficially known as 'Kämpfgruppe Lammerding'). In March, 1944, the group was encircled, with other units of the SS Panzer Korps, and threatened with annihilation. When they were relieved by a counter-attack they were sent to southern France to join the rest of the Division. Das Reich was one of four SS divisions in France at the time of the Allied landings.

In 1943 the Waffen SS was compelled, through heavy losses, to relax its special selectiveness and large numbers of foreigners were recruited or conscripted. By the end of 1944 more than half the Waffen SS were not native Germans. They numbered in their ranks men from both East and West Europe and even from Asia.

In Alsace-Lorraine, in direct contravention of the Armistice terms, all men of military age were conscripted into the German armed forces.

General Lammerding, when on the Russian Front in 1943.

They were told they would be afforded 'the full rights of German nationality'. The Vichy Government protested but was ignored. They didn't make their protest public so the Alsatians believed they had been totally abandoned by the French. Some of the young men got away to Switzerland before they could be called up. Some headed for the 'unoccupied' south of France. Many were caught and shot and their families deported.

On 8 January, 1944, men of Alsace-Lorraine born in 1926 were called up and many of them were directed to the training camps of the Waffen SS. A large number found themselves in Stablack where they were subjected to the rigorous training of the Das Reich Division. Others were given short-term courses in their own country or in German towns near the Rhine and joined the Das Reich Division at Bordeaux. Some recruits were sent direct to Bordeaux.

Command of the Das Reich Division was taken over on 9 December, 1943 by SS Oberführer Heinz Bernard Lammerding who, on 20 April, 1944, was promoted to SS Brigadeführer and Generalmajor of the Waffen SS. Lammerding was born on 27 August, 1905. He was a civil engineer when he joined the SA in 1931 and was employed by the Nazis from October, 1933. He joined the SS in 1935. His various posts included that of commandant of the SS cadet school at Brunswick.

In November, 1939, he joined the Totenkopf (Death's Head) Division as C.O. of the engineer battalion. In 1940 the division closed the Calais pocket. Lammerding was awarded the Iron Cross 1st Class and became C.O. of the Division in 1941 during the early stages of the Russian campaign. He was awarded the Deutsche Kreuz in gold after the Battle of Kharkov.

In the summer of 1943 Himmler created some special anti-terrorist units to combat partisan activity in Russia. In charge of these units was SS Obergruppenführer von dem Bach-Zalewski. Lammerding was his chief of staff. The sort of activity with which he was associated in this role can be judged from one of his last orders. It was addressed to the C.O. of the SS Brigade 'Langemark': 'The inhabitants of Mitkowsky and Klembowka are to be removed from their homes and all resistance will be suppressed. All the dwellings in those areas will be burned and the remains razed by tanks.'

At the beginning of April, 1944, the Das Reich Division, re-equipped and regrouped, left Bordeaux and moved towards the south-east. Headquarters were established at Montauban, between Limoges and Toulouse and the regiments were stationed in the region. They included two Panzergrenadier regiments—Deutchsland and Der Führer. Each had three battalions.

The Division's mission was clear—to maintain the lines of communication at any price. In the event of an Allied landing they were to 'comb' the whole region, seeking and ruthlessly suppressing the Resistance and all who supported it.

On 2 May, the day that Lammerding received the Ritterkreuz for his

54

service on the eastern front, an occasion which was celebrated in the officers' mess at Montauban with champagne and SS songs, a programme of atrocities started. There was a certain similarity about these acts of terror which indicated that they were not spontaneous or the result of individual initiative. The men who carried them out had evidently been specially trained for action against the civilian population. So terrible became their reputation that the people tended to attribute every crime of violence committed by the Germans in that region to the Das Reich Division although in some cases they couldn't have been involved. Hundreds of innocent people were massacred and houses burned. Some of the actions took place near Montauban. At Montpezat de Quercy, for example, the murders included those of a grandfather and his grandchild aged two, who were flung alive into their burning home.

It seems highly improbable that Lammerding was unaware of the excesses of his trained killers. In fact, their style of operation in many places must have been established with his full knowledge.

The pattern was always the same:

(1) The surrounding of the chosen village.
(2) Occupation of the principal offices—police station, town hall, etc.
(3) The rounding up of the population in the village square, often using the town crier to spread the order.

Then came the executions, looting and burning. In at least one place it is recorded that they shut the women and children in the church, but they were later released.

The names of Sturmbannführer Dickmann and Hauptsturmführer Kahn emerge from time to time as the instigators of particularly brutal action, such as that at Frayssinet le Gélat. In this village, when the population of about 400 had been assembled in the square, with the usual brutal 'hurrying up' of the aged and others who didn't move fast enough for their tormentors, a shot was heard. An old woman, terrified by the soldiers, had fired a shotgun. On Dickmann's orders the old lady, aged 80, was dragged out of her house with her two nieces, the other occupants. The three women were hanged before the assembled population. The old woman's body was flung into her blazing home.

Ten men were lined up to be shot. Among them was a lad of 15. His father begged Kahn to let him embrace his son for the last time. Kahn agreed with a mocking laugh and gave the order to fire so that father and son died together.

In these actions, the Division often had the co-operation of the Gestapo and the Militia.

As soon as the news of the Allied landings in Normandy reached the Division they regrouped to carry out their pre-arranged task—moving towards the Normandy front, crushing all resistance en route. Rommel ordered the Division to join Army Group B as quickly as possible.* Armour, which was most urgently needed at the battlefront, was to be sent by rail. Needless to say the Resistance was fully aware of such moves and carried out extensive sabotage of the railways.

The first and third Battalions of the Der Führer Regiment took to the road on 8 June. Their orders were to proceed northwards, stamping out any terrorist activity and putting such fear into the population that they would be too scared to help the Resistance.

In spite of the increased danger the *Maquis* became increasingly active. Apart from railway sabotage, they set ambushes on the roads and succeeded in inflicting losses on the Germans in several places. The SS reaction was typical. They vented their wrath on innocent people, finding the 'terrorists' hard to catch.

The barbarity of the SS towards the civilian population was sanctioned to a certain extent by the German High Command. Keitel sent orders to General von Brodowski, in command of the Clermont-Ferrand region, who passed them to Lammerding. Part of these orders read: 'The atmosphere of insecurity which reigns in the Massif Central must be

---

* When Rommel was told of the Oradour massacre he said the Division should be punished and offered to preside over a court-martial. Hitler, who revered his SS generals, told him it was none of his business.

removed. . . . The civilian population must be made to realize by example that it does not pay them to help the Resistance. The utmost severity must be employed in carrying this out.'

The town of Tulle, south-east of Limoges, was the scene of a clash between the *Maquis* and the Germans. When the SS, commanded by Sturmbannführer Kowatsch, arrived on the scene they organized fearful reprisals for the death of 40 German soldiers. Ninety-nine men were hanged from balconies, trees and lamp-posts in the centre of the town. This was on 9 June.

Lammerding subsequently claimed that he arrived in Tulle on the afternoon of the 9th when the executions had been carried out but, from various eye-witness accounts, it is apparent that he arrived at about 11 am. And there is little doubt that he was the author of an order, rapidly printed and pasted up throughout the town, to the effect that 120 'terrorists' or their accomplices would be hanged as a reprisal for the death of the 40 soldiers, and their bodies flung into the river.

The Gestapo played a leading part in the massacre. Their leader, named Walter, selected the victims from the mass of men aged between 16 and 60 who were rounded up by looking closely at their faces to see if they had shaved and at their feet to see if their shoes were clean. The 'terrorists' were supposed to be a scruffy lot. As the men had been ordered out of their homes at 6 am, few of them had shaved. The actual number of victims was reduced to 99 by the intervention of the Abbé Espinasse who succeeded in convincing Walter that he had killed enough. The hangmen were all volunteers and the appalling spectacle was witnessed as a sort of entertainment by a party of SS sitting at tables at the Tivoli cafe while a gramophone played at full volume. There was much drinking of stolen liquor.

The Das Reich Division established a temporary headquarters in Limoges from 9–11 June. The Der Führer Regiment, commanded by Obersturmführer Stadler, also had its HQ there.

The Tulle massacre on 9 June had no direct bearing on what happened at Oradour the next day, but two incidents which also occurred on the ninth must be associated with Oradour. On 7 June the

FFI* launched an attack on the German garrison at Guérat, to the north-east of Limoges. In a few hours they overcame the Germans and captured the town. The next day the Germans launched a counter-attack, using aircraft and machine-gunning the streets. They were repulsed. On 9 June, after another aerial attack, the Wehrmacht succeeded in regaining control. Lammerding sent the third Battalion of the Der Führer Regiment, commanded by Sturmbannführer Helmut Kämpfe, to take charge of the situation in Guérat.

On its way there the 9th company met four lorries carrying young *maquisards*, few of whom were armed. The SS lined up 29 of them and shot them by the roadside. Seven more, encountered farther on, were also shot.

Kämpfe decided to leave a detachment of his SS to help the Wehrmacht take control of the town again. The rest of the third Battalion turned round and started back to Limoges. They took with them about 20 prisoners who were added to other prisoners in Limoges taken at Tulle and all were eventually deported to Germany.

Kämpfe was in a hurry to get back to Limoges and did something that was amazing for such an experienced, efficient officer. He drove on alone, ahead of his men by about three kilometres. But for this rash act Oradour might have been saved.

Night was falling and Kämpfe saw the lights of a vehicle ahead signalling him to stop. This vehicle carried a group of *Maquis* under a Sergeant Jean Canou, a miner from St Léonard. Here is his account of what happened:

> We were returning from blowing up a bridge at Brignac. There were eight or ten of us in a small truck armed with sub-machine guns, grenades and revolvers. It was almost dark when we saw a car approaching. Our driver signalled it to stop and our men ran to the car as it came to a halt. We were surprised to see that the driver, who was alone, was in German uniform. He was unarmed and made no

* French Forces of the Interior.

effort to resist. We put him in our truck and soon left the main road taking the road to Moisanne. The German was a tall, handsome type who laughed when we arrested him. Just as we turned off the main road we heard other vehicles passing. We handed the prisoner over to our chiefs and I didn't see him again.

Kämpfe probably laughed when he was taken prisoner because he thought they would soon come face to face with his men and he would be freed. He had not foreseen the truck turning down a side road.

The SS came across their CO's empty car with the motor still running. The *Maquis* had not taken it with them because only one of them could drive. The soldiers spread out in search of their chief. They fetched everyone out of their houses in the hamlet of La Bussière and searched every building to no avail.

They returned to the scene from Limoges at 11 pm accompanied by a party of militiamen. At the entrance to La Bussière they burst into a farmhouse and the militiamen questioned the farmer about his livestock—how many sheep, cattle and pigs he had. No questions about Kämpfe. Finally the farmer was shoved outside and shot. A neighbouring farmer suffered the same fate. In the end the SS returned to Limoges with no news of the vanished officer.

Kämpfe's disappearance had a shattering effect on his fellow officers in Limoges and the news quickly spread through the division. He was a personal friend of Lammerding who burst into a towering rage. He regarded him as one of his most valuable officers.

Kämpfe, who was 35, was a popular soldier with a distinguished military career. He had fought valiantly in Russia and was awarded the Ritterkreuz. He had previously received the Iron Cross classes 1 and 2. It is important to note that he was also a great personal friend of Otto Dickmann.

The incident was recorded in the SS records as 'disappeared in the south of France while in action against terrorists.' What actually happened to Kämpfe is not clear. He was never seen again although it was reported on 28 June that he was a prisoner of the *Maquis* at

Cheissoux. It is believed that he was shot while trying to escape.

The other occurrence which had an important bearing on the Oradour massacre was the blowing up of the railway line crossing the viaduct over the River Vienne near St Junien, about six miles south-west of Oradour on the morning of 8 June. A locomotive and several wagons were derailed and part of the train fell into the river. It was the work of a small group of *Maquis*. Although goods traffic was disrupted, passengers were able to complete their journey by getting out of a train on one side of the viaduct and walking over the bridge—which was largely undamaged—to board another train.

On the night of 8 June, ten armed Wehrmacht soldiers travelling from Angoulême to Limoges were among the passengers who had to walk over the viaduct. The *Maquis*, who were hidden in a wood at the side of the track, opened fire and killed two of the soldiers. Five of them ran back to the train they had left and returned to Angoulême. The other three went on to Limoges with the bodies of their dead comrades. They 'phoned their Limoges headquarters before they set out and an assorted bunch of Wehrmacht was immediately despatched to St Junien by a special train. They were accompanied by Obersturmführer Wickers of the Gestapo and an interpreter named Hübsch. Half-way to St Junien the train was stopped at a station for Hübsch to telephone to the stationmaster there, ordering him to alert the Mayor and the chief of police to meet the train with plans of the town.

When the Germans arrived, Wickers had these officials frisked and locked in separate rooms at the station while the soldiers prepared to resist a *Maquis* attack. Wickers questioned the Mayor and police chief separately. It was reported that the Mayor was asked if there were any terrorists or partisans in the town and he replied, 'Yes. At least 1,800'. This extraordinary statement, which was quite untrue, could well have saved the town (which had a population of 10,000) from severe reprisals. The Germans didn't want another battle at that stage. Their big fight was awaiting them in the north.

Wickers ordered that 100 men from the town should assemble on the 9th with picks and shovels to dig trenches for defensive purposes. Fifty actually turned up, most of them aged. They worked for four hours and were then released.

At about 10 am on the 9th Wickers was informed by the Limoges Gestapo headquarters that the SS would be coming to relieve the Wehrmacht. At about 10.30 the 1st Battalion of the Der Führer Regiment, commanded by Sturmbannführer Dickmann, arrived from Rochechouart. They immediately raided a number of garages, stealing as much petrol as they could carry away. They subsequently terrified the population by indulging in grenade-throwing exercises in the centre of the town. Dickmann set up his headquarters at the Hôtel de la Gare and stayed there overnight.

On the morning of 10 June, Dickmann received an urgent summons to go to Limoges where he learned of the disappearance of his friend Kämpfe. He had an interview with his regimental C.O., Obersturmbannführer Stadler. Action for the recovery of Kämpfe and possible reprisals were undoubtedly discussed. There are two versions of what was decided. One states that while the region to the north and north-east of Limoges was scoured for the missing officer a 'zone of reprisals' should be established to the west, extending over 30 kms. The idea was to avoid a clash of the two exercises. The other version is that Dickmann received Stadler's approval to operate in the region of Oradour with a view to trying to contact the Resistance. He would take hostages with him to use for bargaining for the release of Kämpfe. From what happened subsequently, it appears that the former version is probably the true one. Anyway, it is apparent that Dickmann returned to St Junien that morning with approval from both Stadler and Lammerding to take a certain line of action.

Dickmann was accompanied on the return journey by Oberscharführer Joachim Kleist of the Gestapo, renowned for his brutality, and a Gestapo interpreter named Eugene Patry. There were also four members of the Militia, led by a man named Pitrud. The convoy was preceded by a truckload of Wehrmacht soldiers and followed by three lorries full of provisions for the SS.

The party went to the Hôtel de la Gare and it was there, on a table in the dining room, that the destruction of Oradour was planned. The conference started at about 10.30 am. It is presumed that Dickmann presided and others present probably included Kahn, accompanied by other officers, Kleist the Gestapo man and the militiamen for whom Patry acted as interpreter. The Frenchmen were there to provide local knowledge. It is obvious from the mechanical way in which much of the raid was carried out that the SS were well briefed about the village, which they had never visited before. It is likely that they had an ordnance survey map.

At 11.30 the meeting broke up and towards noon 120 men of the third company—which had a total complement of 180—were told to prepare for action. Eight lorries, two armoured tracked vehicles (schützpanzerwagen)—for chasing people over the countryside—and a motor cycle were lined up. Ordnance included four heavy machine guns, 24 light machine guns and 15 machine pistols, apart from rifles and revolvers.

The third company were specialists in explosives and incendiary devices which is probably why they were chosen for the task. They took what was needed to burn a village and to asphyxiate a large number of people in a building of moderate size. The detachment included a number of Alsatians. They took their places in the lorries with the Germans, prepared for another punitive expedition. However, the men were given a hint that this action was going to be something special when a junior officer, Untersturmbannführer Barth, passed among them remarking, 'Today you're going to see the blood flow.' and adding, as a sort of afterthought, 'We're also going to see what the Alsatians are capable of doing.'

The convoy set out at 1.30 pm. Oradour was only about six miles away but they did not take the direct route (see map). They travelled east on the road which runs parallel to the River Vienne then swung north to enter Oradour at the lower end. This was evidently a tactical move to facilitate the rapid occupation and surrounding of the village. The direct route from St Junien enters Oradour half-way up the main street. The convoy turned north at St Victurnien and not far from the point where the road joins the Oradour-Limoges road Dickmann called

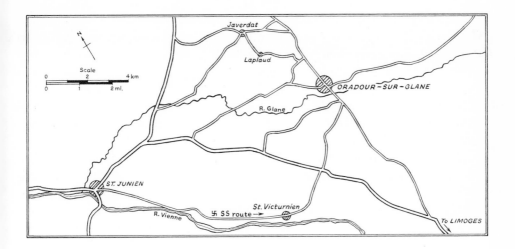

a halt. He ordered the officers and NCOs to gather round him. They were given a final briefing and some papers (possibly maps) were distributed. The militiamen were not there. Neither was Kleist, the Gestapo man, who had left St Junien for an operation at Saillat.

From the survivors' accounts we know what happened when the convoy arrived at Oradour. But the motivation of the men who did the dirty work was only partly revealed at the trial at Bordeaux in 1953. Some facts are clear. The men were urged to 'get on with the job' by the officers and NCOs and there was taunting of the Alsatians. Liquor was widely looted but the assassins didn't have time to fortify themselves during the operation. They drank afterwards and went off singing towards Nieul.

Motivated by the blind obedience to orders which had been instilled in them in their training, and fear of the consequences should they show any sign of failure to carry out the butchery to which they were assigned, the men worked like automatons, squeezing triggers, hurling grenades and starting fires.

A terrible madness must have seized them as they fired wildly into the screaming mass of women and children in the church. They were under orders to kill every living soul and this they did—or thought they did. They used hundreds of bullets for this part of the slaughter. The floor of the church near the main entrance was littered with empty cases.

It was Kahn who fired the machine gun as a signal for the execution of the men and both he and Dickmann were always in the thick of things, giving orders.

One of the many questions which arise is whether the killing of the whole population was intended when the raid was planned at St Junien. Kleist is reported to have told one of the militiamen after the conference that 40 hostages were going to be killed at Oradour that afternoon and he wanted no part of it—strange for a Gestapo man. So how did the enormous increase in the death toll come about? Is it possible that Lammerding, despite subsequent protestations of non-involvement, radioed the change of plan to Dickmann en route? Witnesses said that Dickmann, who rode at the head of the convoy, was wearing earphones and seemed to be in communication with someone by radio. It could be that the slaughter mushroomed of its own accord. Certainly towards the end it seemed as if the officers were afraid of leaving a single witness to what they had done and kept driving the men to more and more excesses.

But why Oradour? This is the most baffling question of all. There are many theories from various sources. Here is a selection, followed in each case by comments based on my own research:

(1) General von Brodowski, commanding the Clermont-Ferrand region was, according to a Press report, carrying a diary when he was captured on 16 October, 1944. This was the entry for 11 June, 1944: 'In the course of an action on the 10th, Oradour and its environs (31 kms south-west of Limoges) were reduced to ashes.' Then the entry for 14 June: 'Regarding Oradour—30 kms south-west of Limoges—a French version has been received: 600 people perished. An Untersturmführer of the SS armoured Division Das Reich had been taken prisoner at Nieul

(8 kms north-west of Limoges) and transported to Oradour. He managed to escape. The body of a paymaster class one bearing traces of handcuffs was subsequently found. The whole of the male population of Oradour has been shot. The women and children took refuge in the church. The church caught fire. Explosives had been stored in the church. The women and children also perished.'

There is considerable doubt about the authenticity of these diary entries. See (6) for another version of the 'prisoner' story. Oradour-sur-Glane is north-west, not south-west, of Limoges. Which could support the next—the most popular theory . . .

(2) The wrong Oradour was attacked. South-west of Limoges lies the village of Oradour-sur-Vayres where *Maquis* activity had been reported. Raymond Carter, in his book *Le Scandale d'Oradour*, underlines the 'wrong Oradour' theory. He quotes a former Resistance leader who told him that the *Maquis* ambushed a detachment of the Das Reich division near Oradour-sur-Vayres in reprisal for the atrocities they had carried out elsewhere. There were many casualties on both sides. In revenge the SS decided to wipe out the village and sent an execution squad to the wrong Oradour.

I am convinced there was no mistake. The killers knew exactly where they were going and were helped by people who knew the region well. They were pressed for time, being under orders to move north, and knew Oradour-sur-Glane would be an easy target. They did not want to lose more men in another clash with the Resistance.

(3) It was a reprisal for an ambush near Oradour-sur-Glane. In a book entitled *Crimes Ennemis en France, Oradour-sur-Glane* (*Archives du Service de Recherche des Crimes de Guerre Ennemis*) it is stated that an SS deserter said his unit had been ambushed by the *Maquis* about 15 kms from Oradour-sur-Glane. Four SS men were wounded and Dickmann, who was leading the unit, decided that the next village they came to should suffer severe reprisals.

I put this to the Mayor of the new Oradour, Dr Robert Lapuelle,* who was in St Junien as a young medical student at the time. He completely refuted the idea and all accounts of the movements of the 1st Battalion of the Der Führer Regiment give no support to the theory. Colonel Rousselier, commander of the 12th military region of the FFI at Limoges, stressed: 'There were no engagements of any sort in the region of Oradour-sur-Glane. We had no camp, no arms cache and no explosives anywhere near the village.'

(4) Otto Dickmann's personal record of the action reads: 'On 10/6 at 1330 hours the 1st Battalion SS "DF" surrounded Oradour. After a search the village was burned. Munitions were found in almost every house. On 11/6 two companies marched on Nieul-le-Château. The terrorists had evacuated the locality during the night. Total casualties—548 enemy dead, one of our men wounded.' According to Obersturmbannführer Wardinger, who succeeded Stadler as C.O. of the Der Führer Regiment when the latter was promoted to command the Hohenstaufen Division, Dickmann returned to Limoges on the night of the 10th and told Stadler that his men had been fired on as soon as they reached Oradour. They had to retaliate and in the course of the exchange some buildings caught fire. The flames spread rapidly and general destruction occurred when caches of arms exploded.

This is ridiculous.

(5) A French historian, not a local man, told me that the real reason, which had been hushed up, was that two German motor-cyclists had been found dead in a ditch, horribly mutilated, near Oradour.

There is nothing to support this theory. If it were true the inhabitants would have been fearful of reprisals and tried to flee when the SS arrived. All accounts point to their air of innocence throughout.

---

* Dr Lapuelle, who repeatedly said 'There was no reason for the massacre', was due to take an exam in Limoges on 10 June, 1944 but thought better of it when he saw the SS movements. A friend, a veterinary student, who ventured towards Oradour was held in a ditch at gunpoint for several hours.

(6) A German report said an officer and his driver had been attacked near Oradour. The officer was Obersturmführer Gerlach who had gone to Nieul on 9 June to prepare billets. He had returned to Limoges at dawn on the 10th half-naked and without his driver. He reported that they had been captured, stripped and transported by lorry as far as the entrance to Oradour. They had been made to run the gauntlet of the villagers, particularly the women. He had got away but his driver had been killed.

No one believes this story today. It would have been another instance in which reprisals would have been anticipated.

(7) Kleist, the Gestapo man, is reported to have told his associates that hostages were to be shot in Oradour as a reprisal for a *Maquis* attack on an SS vehicle. The 12 soldiers in it had been captured and taken to Oradour where all were hanged except an officer who escaped.

Probably a distorted version of the previous story.

(8) Two authoritative American books on the history of the Waffen SS give the same reason for the massacre. George H. Stein in his book *The Waffen SS, Hitler's Elite Guard at War* (Oxford University Press 1966) says, 'As elements of the Division (Das Reich) passed near the village of Oradour-sur-Glane a French resistance sniper shot and killed an officer.' In *Uniforms, Organization and History of the Waffen SS* by R. J. Bender and H. P. Taylor (published by Bender), we find, 'As the Division passed near the village of Oradour-sur-Glane a French sniper shot and killed an SS captain.'

If one is to believe all other accounts of the movements of the Das Reich Division this theory is ridiculous. And one only has to see the narrow, winding lanes in the Oradour area to realize what a tangle an armoured division in a hurry would get into. Besides, anyone shooting at such a terrifying mass of men and machines would have to be mad.

(9) Monsieur Chaintron, a former Prefect of Haute Vienne —the region in which Oradour is located—writes in the preface to *Oradour-sur-Glane, Vision d'Epouvante*, published by the *Association*

Nationale des Familles des Martyrs d'Oradour-sur-Glane, that the object of the massacre was to terrorize the mass of the people in the region to discourage them from supporting the Resistance and to illustrate beyond doubt that the Germans were still all-powerful.

There is a certain amount of truth in this, yet no attempt was made by the SS to publicize the exploit as an example of what might happen elsewhere. In fact, efforts were made to conceal the evidence, e.g. the half-hearted burial attempts and the search by the Gestapo for survivors who might tell the horrible story.

(10) It was a reprisal for the capture of Sturmbannführer Kämpfe.

This, I believe, is true. I believe that the massacre was mainly conceived by Otto Dickmann. This is supported by the letter from Lammerding to the Bordeaux tribunal in which he asserted that Dickmann 'exceeded his orders'. One assumes that Dickmann received approval from Lammerding and Stadler for some sort of reprisal raid in response to the capture of Kämpfe, the details being left to him.

SS Brigadeführer (Major-General) Kurt Meyer, the first German war criminal to be condemned to death by the Allies (the sentence was later commuted) claimed that 'the SS committed no crimes except the massacre at Oradour, and that was the action of a single man. He was scheduled to go before a court-martial but died a hero's death before he could be tried.'

Oradour was probably selected for destruction because it was an easy target with no resistance, easy to surround, and because it lay between St Junien and Nieul where billets for the night had been arranged for the 1st Battalion. Dickmann was in a raging temper as a result of the loss of his friend Kämpfe. He and Kahn whipped up a bloodlust in their men and themselves took part in the killing.

The war diary of the Der Führer Regiment suggests that Oradour was selected arbitrarily as an easy target 'largely to improve the sagging morale of the troops'.

The fact that the success of the reprisal was not widely publicized by the Germans, as may have been the original intention, with a view to instilling fear into the local population, suggests that the monstrous reality of what they had done dawned on the killers afterwards and it was decided to keep quiet about it. This is probably why the Gestapo sought the survivors and why efforts were made to inter some of the bodies.

So there it is: A furious officer, used to killing innocent people, looking for a place on which he could vent his wrath for the loss of his friend without wasting too much time (the Division was under orders to get to the Normandy front as quickly as possible), advised by local people who knew the country between St Junien and Nieul and may well have recommended Oradour, followed by a mad mass slaughter about which there were second thoughts when the deed had been done.

Now let us see how much of this is borne out by the Bordeaux trial.

4 The Trial

In January, 1953, eight and a half years after the massacre, a trial took place in Bordeaux. It was officially known as 'L'Affaire Kahn et Autres', but to the world it was the Oradour Trial. It was rocked by politics, punctuated with outbursts and, in the end, none of the accused was executed.

In the years following the end of the war in Europe the Oradour massacre tended to be overshadowed by the various international developments. It was even rejected with the popular French comment 'C'est la guerre'.

But the survivors and the relatives of the victims could not forget in spite of the soft soap of national recognition of their sacrifice in the form of the Croix de Guerre for the monument to the dead and the légion d'Honneur conferred on the village during yet another ministerial visit.

State funds were provided to build a barracks-type village near the ruins and plans were drawn up for 'a magnificent new Oradour'. The ruins were classified as an historic monument and taken over by the Beaux Arts. The dead received the ultimate accolade: 'Morts pour La France'.

However, the Association Nationale des Familles des Martyrs was far from appeased. They clamoured for the tracing of the guilty and their being brought to trial. But this was not easy with the SS survivors scattered and hiding in a divided Germany. Seven Germans had been arrested and identified as having taken part. But what about the rest?

One difficulty was that the law in France and in certain other countries at that time was that no ex-serviceman could be punished for something he had been ordered to do by a superior officer, however criminal that act might be.

It was soon established that men from Alsace-Lorraine had taken part in the massacre. But how could one accuse anyone from a country which had suffered so much under the Nazi yoke? Altogether 130,000 young men from that country had been forcibly enrolled in the German forces and 42,000 had been killed or were missing. Those who were conscripted or managed to escape from the Nazis formed the Association of Deserters, Escapees and Forced Recruits. It was this body which rallied to defend the 14 Alsatians who were eventually added to the list of men for trial.

The deplorable part of the Bordeaux trial was that of the 21 who faced the judges none was an officer. The highest rank was that of Oberscharführer or senior warrant officer.

Of the Alsatians, two had served in the French Army from 1939–40. Six had deserted from the SS in Normandy and surrendered to the British. They told of the Oradour massacre and, after interrogation by French officers, enlisted in the FFI. Two of these subsequently served with the French Army in Indo-China.

Between 1945 and 1948 eight of the Alsatians had been interrogated from time to time as witnesses of the massacre. Between times they carried on their normal civilian occupations in Alsace. It was not until three weeks before the opening of the trial that the 14 Alsatians were arrested and charged under a law of 1948 which created an offence of 'collective responsibility'.

One of them was immediately regarded as a traitor. He was a sergeant who had volunteered to serve in the SS. Most of them had been between the ages of 17 and 19 when they took part in the massacre.

As soon as the accusations were announced the people of Alsace-Lorraine protested violently. They maintained that the young men concerned were as innocent as the people who had been killed in Oradour. They were all victims of the Nazis. They pointed to what had happened to the young men who had evaded conscription. If they were caught they were shot. In any case, caught or not, their families suffered deportation. They pointed to the Gauleiter who was appointed to rule

Alsace-Lorraine, Robert Wagner. He had compelled the young men to enlist in the German forces and had been shot for his crimes. All the Alsatians who were conscripted were the victims of that evil man and it was utterly unjust to accuse any of them of actions for which they were not responsible, actions which they could not avoid without losing their own lives.

Two years before the Bordeaux trial General Lammerding had been judged in his absence by the same tribunal for his part in the hangings at Tulle and condemned to death. At the time of the Oradour trial he was living in Düsseldorf in the British zone, where he was carrying on his old profession of civil engineer. The French Government asked the British to extradite him so that he could be brought to the tribunal. It was subsequently reported that Lammerding and his wife had left their home for an unknown destination, but neither the British nor the German authorities made any apparent effort to find them. Eventually it became known that they had taken refuge in Schleswig-Holstein. Lammerding was finally traced to Wiesbaden in the American zone. Thereafter interest was lost in him. The British reluctance to extradite Lammerding was based on their decision in 1948 to extradite no one from their zone 'except where a charge of murder could be proved beyond any doubt', and this involved a detailed accusation confirmed by numerous witnesses.

One of the sensations of the Oradour trial was the arrival of a letter from Lammerding in which he claimed that both he and Stadler (who was also known to be alive at that time) knew nothing of the massacre until it was over. The accused, he said, should be acquitted because they could do nothing other than obey Dickmann's orders and Dickmann himself had 'exceeded his orders'. To prove the authenticity of his letter, Lammerding had his signature witnessed by a solicitor.

A number of German newspapers were critical of his behaviour. A Frankfurt paper stated that Herr Lammerding was formerly the chief of a group which claimed to represent the ideals of fidelity and virility. Yet when the men he commanded were in a difficult situation at Bordeaux surely his place should have been with them? Shouldn't he have hastened to support them and avoided any suggestion of extradition?

In 1965 Lammerding came into the news again when he sued a German journalist who had dared to recall, in an article, that he had been condemned to death in France for executing hostages.

His accusation reiterated his plea of innocence in the Tulle and Oradour affairs. He sheltered behind dead men—Kowatsch who he said was responsible for the Tulle hangings, and Dickmann whose initiative led to the Oradour massacre. It is worth noting that he never accused Kahn who was believed to be still alive somewhere in Sweden. His action failed.

In accordance with the custom at that time, the Bordeaux tribunal was a military one. It was composed of six officers who had been active in the Resistance and a presiding civilian judge—in this case Monsieur Nussy Saint-Saens—who managed to keep control of the court despite exceptionally awkward circumstances.

The president stressed at the outset that it was really the Nazi régime that was on trial. Everyone was horrified by the massacre and wondered how it could possibly have occurred. His answer, and he would underline it, was that it happened because some beings who had lost all traces of human dignity were bent on establishing by force a completely materialistic order. It was their blind obedience to the totalitarian state which had brought about this terrible thing.

The president had to curb many demonstrations in the courtroom, principally by the relatives of the dead and the survivors who sat in a group towards the front of the court.

The accommodation was primitive and overcrowded. The accused were divided into two groups, the Germans on one side, the Alsatians on the other. They sat bunched together on wooden benches.

When the indictment was read at the preliminary hearing everyone in the court rose. The bereaved wept. The accused maintained an expression of indifference.

One of the Germans, a man named Nobbe, admitted having taken part in all the atrocities at Oradour. He pleaded guilty to all the accusations. But he was proved to be mentally ill and was sent to a hospital.

The principal defence counsel for the Alsatians was Maître Strecken-berg, chief advocate of Strasbourg, and the people of his country regarded him as representing all of them.

Another defending lawyer from Alsace described the burden that country had had to bear during the Nazi occupation. He vividly recalled how every effort had been made to wipe out the French influence. No one was allowed to speak the language. Children had been conscripted into the Hitler Youth Movement and the young men into the German armed forces.

The trial lasted a month. The terrible stories of the survivors, especially that of Madame Rouffanche, engendered a great deal of emotion and there was much use of handkerchiefs as well as outbursts of indignation. The prisoners' accounts of their roles in the killing conformed to a pattern after a while. They had 'forgotten' a great deal of what had occurred. Several maintained that if they were forced to fire at people they aimed to miss. The Alsatians claimed they had been 'bullied' into their actions by the officers and NCOs. Prominent among the latter was Sergeant Boos, the volunteer Alsatian.

One of the Germans, named Pfeffer, who admitted killing people, said Kahn had made them do it. He was among those who herded a group of men into a barn and used his machine gun on them. He had aimed at their chests.

Frenzel, another German, said the officers stood behind the firing squads. He also accused Kahn who, he said, personally took part in killing the wounded.

Lenz, the German warrant officer, claimed that he took no part in the massacre. He said he spent the afternoon walking round the village. But he was contradicted by Sergeant Boos who said Lenz had ordered the men to toss concentrated charges (explosive wrapped round grenades) into the houses. Lenz, he said, had definitely taken part in the shootings and had tossed grenades among the women and children in the church.

One of the Alsatians, Daul, said they had been told at St Junien that they were going to a town to free Sturmbannführer Kämpfe. He had been a member of a machine-gun crew positioned near a farm outside

Some of the twenty-one accused at the Bordeaux tribunal.

the village. They had been ordered to prevent people from entering or leaving the village. They had turned back a girl on a bicycle who had tried to get into Oradour, also a woman with a shopping bag and a man who wanted to pick up his tobacco ration. Later a music professor from Limoges argued with them and they allowed him to go into Oradour to talk to an officer. When he went into the village he saw Boos shooting people. Other prisoners also described how Kahn took an active part in the massacre. An Alsatian appropriately named Elsässer said one of the women in the church who tried to get out had shouted to Kahn in German that she was not French and should not be treated like the others. Kahn had shoved her back into the flames saying he wanted no witnesses of what was happening.

Josef Busch (Alsatian) admitted being a member of the execution squad at the Desourteaux garage. He thought some of the victims were still alive when they were covered with brushwood and other material, but he wasn't sure. He was later sent down to the church to make sure no one escaped. He saw two women approach, asking after their children. Boos and a German shoved them into a barn opposite the church, where a group of men had died, and shot them.

Graff, another Alsatian, said he was in a field at the edge of the village with a German and a Russian when they saw two women hiding in a hedge. The women started to scream and they shot them. The bodies were taken in a wheelbarrow to one of the burning buildings. Graff said he was ordered to the church where he helped to carry brushwood inside. He heaped it on the bodies of the women and children. There was much screaming and groaning. One woman and a child who tried to get away were clubbed to death by a soldier. The church was full of soldiers at that time. They were under orders.

One man, Höchlinger, an Alsatian, claimed he hid in a hedge outside the village throughout the afternoon and had actually gone to sleep.

A German, Daab, told of the deployment of the troops when they entered the village. The first platoon went directly up the main street while the second and third spread out to surround it. He denied taking part in any of the executions and claimed he spent the time guarding the trucks.

Albert Ochs, an Alsatian who served in the FFI after deserting in Normandy, said he was conscripted in the SS in early 1944. His brother-in-law had refused and been shot. He said a German sergeant named Steger had ordered the men to get all the people out of the houses. Anyone who refused or was bedridden was to be shot.

Ochs said he didn't shoot anyone but he saw the sergeant and another German shoving an elderly invalid woman out of her home. He told them to leave her alone and Steger had shouted, 'Shut up, Alsatian!' They shot her in her own doorway. He was hit in the legs by ricochets and taken away for treatment by a medical orderly.

Grienberger (German) said he was in an execution squad but deliberately fired high. He deserted in Normandy.

One of the accused showed genuine remorse for what he had been involved in. He was an Alsatian named Antoine Löhner, white-haired and soft-spoken. He had been conscripted in the Waffen SS in 1943 and deserted in Normandy. He said he had helped to round up the people at Oradour on the orders of Sergeant Steger. He had acted as interpreter for Kahn and interrogated Dr Desourteaux when he arrived at the Champ de Foire. Steger's squad took a party of men to the Denys coachhouse. Among them was an old priest. After the executions Steger set fire to the building and they moved on down to the church.

Löhner said he saw Boos shoot two women in the doorway of the barn opposite the church. He himself had to carry brushwood into the church. He was still haunted by the screams of the women and children. He saw Boos throw grenades among them. Before the detachment left for Nieul, Kahn distributed wine and spirits. Löhner said he was one of the men who returned to Oradour to bury some of the dead.

The supposed villain of the piece, Sergeant Boos, said he joined the SS in 1942 and was awarded the Iron Cross and the Russian Service Medal. Boos said the Oradour raid was planned by the officers. He just obeyed orders throughout the whole affair. Kahn was 'a hard man'. They had been told about Kämpfe at St Junien and had been told to expect 'heavy fighting' where they were going. Boos admitted leading the last group of men to execution. He also admitted being in the church but couldn't remember clearly what happened there. He denied the allegation that he had shot two women in a barn opposite the church. He also denied firing a machine gun in the church. He maintained that the other accused were saying things about him because they wanted revenge.

Boos was asked if he went to a bakery and after a long pause said he couldn't remember. The firebox of a bakery oven in which the remains of an eight-week-old baby were discovered was produced in court. Boos refused to reply to all questions about the incident.

So many of the accused claimed that they couldn't remember what had happened or that they had fired to miss, or weren't even in the village at the time that the presiding judge was moved to remark at one stage, 'The court finds it difficult to understand how anyone at all was killed at Oradour.'

Sergeant Boos.

The picture that emerged from the prisoners' responses was that of a company of frightened, brainwashed men jumping to orders from furious, brutal officers and NCOs. The men had dashed about in response to commands without having a clear picture of what the exercise was all about. When the presiding judge asked if there were any among them who were truly repentant for what they had done only three stood up.

The prosecution witnesses included the survivors from the Laudy barn who couldn't identify any of the accused. Not unnaturally in the heat and fear of the moment the features of any individual executioner had not lingered in their memories. Besides, the machine-gunners were standing with their backs to the light at the entrance to the barn. In their camouflaged tunics and helmets they all looked alike.

A number of the witnesses pointed out that their sole aim that afternoon had been to get out of the way of the soldiers, not to concentrate on their faces. Besides it was over eight years ago. In any case they couldn't understand why they should have to identify any of the accused. They had been SS men and had admitted being at Oradour that day. Surely that was enough to convict them?

Dr Masfrand, custodian of the ruins at that time, produced a number of articles found there including a spectacle case and cigarette case perforated by bullets which had certainly not been fired to miss their owners.

During the testimony of the prosecution witnesses there was trouble when it was learned that the French National Assembly had repealed the 1948 Act of 'collective responsibility'. The effect in the courtroom was dramatic. The survivors and the bereaved refused to sit down. A Monsieur Brouillaud, president of the Association of the Families of the Martyrs, addressed the judges. He maintained that the deputies had by their action approved the massacre. The bereaved were now afraid the killers would be reprieved. This could not be tolerated. He was ordered to sit down. He refused. He was threatened with expulsion from the courtroom. There was general commotion. The Oradour people blocked the exists. The Press joined in the shouting.

The presiding judge eventually restored order by promising that any of the accused who were found guilty would be punished in accordance with the penal code.

There was a demonstration outside the courtroom as well and speeches were made, including one by the Mayor of Bordeaux who wore a tricolor sash. He promised that the orphans of Oradour would be adopted by the city, overlooking the fact that nearly all the children had perished in the church.

Summing up for the prosecution, Lieut.-Colonel Gardon said it was incredible that so many people had been killed by so small a company of men. He appreciated that the Alsatians had been recruited by force but demanded their punishment as 'unintentional criminals'—but criminals just the same.

'The Germans at Oradour were our enemies,' he stressed, 'but the others were actually Frenchmen and they killed their brothers and sisters.'

One could not overlook the fact that they had been young at the time and under orders, but they should have been influenced by an example of true courage which was displayed that afternoon. Dr Desourteaux, the Mayor of Oradour, had offered himself as a hostage—and later his family too—to save his fellow villagers. The National Assembly had honoured his memory only a few days before and the whole French nation was in admiration of this mayor who had shown how fear need not prevent a man of honour from offering his life to save others.

Turning to the accused Alsatians, he said he had only noticed signs of emotion among them when the plight of their country under Nazi occupation had been described. Otherwise they had appeared singularly indifferent and unmoved by the account of the death of a French village, a village they had helped to exterminate.

Colonel Garden called for sentences of hard labour for all of them except Sergeant Boos. He deserved to die.

'Messieurs les juges,' he concluded, 'if you find the accused not guilty it will imply that on 10 June, 1944 at Oradour-sur-Glane, in spite of the human remains and in spite of the ruins which the whole world can see, the population was not exterminated nor was the village destroyed.'

The principal defence counsel, le Bâtonnier Moliérac, pleaded that the accused had been young men robbed of all individuality and personality. Were such men intellectually capable of refusing to obey orders from the SS officers and NCOs in the face of the rest of the company?

He cited Jackson, the US prosecutor at the Nuremberg Trial, who had said one could not expect the inferior ranks to ponder on the legality of an order. One had to remember that a soldier had but one function, to obey orders no matter how sickening might be the outcome. The accused were not at Oradour to have a conscience but to carry out their orders. Every army unit was wrapped inescapably in a mantle of discipline. They submitted to orders and to a certain intellectual superiority in those who gave them. They were, in fact, nothing more than an execution squad in both senses of the expression. The accused didn't feel they were guilty. They saw themselves as trapped beasts and really didn't know how they could have got out of doing the things of which they were accused. They would have had to be superhuman.

The trial, he went on, was basically that of a totalitarian régime. The chief culprits, the promoters of Nazism—many of whom were still alive—could not be brought before them that day so their dupes, their first victims, were made answerable. The accused were not the real culprits. One had to go higher up the ladder of responsibility. When the time came to review the history of the period, the supreme head of the Nazi régime would be seen to bear responsibility not only for victims such as those at Oradour but also for the men who carried out his commands.

'It was he who put these men in uniform,' he concluded. 'It was he who held them in the vice of discipline and, after blacking out their intellect, led them by degrees to be involved in the most appalling bestialities.'

The magistrates retired to consider their verdict on 12 February at 5 pm. They returned to the courtroom at 2 pm the following day.

Of the Germans, Lenz, the warrant officer, was sentenced to death. One of them, Degenhardt, was acquitted and the others were sentenced to terms of imprisonment varying from 10 to 12 years, most with hard labour. Forty-two other Germans, tried in their absence, were condemned to death.

Among the Alsatians, Boos was sentenced to death, nine others were sentenced to prison with hard labour and the remaining four to prison. No sentence exceeded eight years.

When the sentences were announced there was a great outburst of indignation throughout France. They were considered utterly inadequate for such a terrible crime. There was a protest march through Limoges in which 50,000 people are said to have taken part. Notices were displayed reading: 'WE WILL NOT ACCEPT THE VERDICT.'

On the other hand, the people of Alsace-Lorraine went into mourning over the injustice of the sentences on their countrymen. They were too severe. The mayors of all the towns in Alsace walked in silent procession past the war memorial in Strasbourg. The Bishop of Strasbourg advocated the non-acceptance of the sentences.

Meanwhile in Paris the legislature discussed an amnesty proposal and on 19 February the amnesty law was passed by 319 votes to 211, with 88 deputies abstaining. The Upper House gave approval by 176 votes to 79.

The sentenced Alsatians, with the exception of Boos, were driven back to their country in secret. Five of the seven Germans were also repatriated, their sentences being less than the eight years they had been detained awaiting trial. In 1954, the two men who were condemned to death had their sentences commuted to hard labour.

Oradour, of course, felt outraged. The mayor removed the Croix de Guerre from the Town Hall in the new village and the president of the Association of Families of the Martyrs removed the Légion d'Honneur from the cemetery. At the main entrance to the ruins two notice boards were put up. One bore the names of the Alsatians who had been sentenced and the part that each was said to have taken in the massacre. The other listed the parliamentarians who had voted for the amnesty. The list of Alsatians was headed: 'The monsters listed here took part in the murder of 642 inhabitants of Oradour-sur-Glane. These are their names and the crimes they committed . . .' And at the end of the list was inscribed: 'Thanks to the amnesty law these criminals are free.'

The parliamentarians' list was headed: 'These 319 deputies pardoned the SS monsters who murdered, burned and pillaged in Oradour-sur-Glane . . .' A list of names followed. Then came: 'These senators confirmed the deputies' vote . . .' followed by more names.

The boards remained there until 1966.

Conclusion

Considered in relation to other massacres in the Second World War, Oradour may seem to be a minor affair. When one thinks of Hiroshima, Dresden, Katyn, the concentration camps and similar scenes of massive carnage Oradour may not seem so terrible.

What makes Oradour unique is the slaughter of 642 people for no apparent reason on a sunny summer afternoon—the personalized killing to a timetable. The whole affair was worked out with typical SS thoroughness and would have gone without a hitch if the women and children had been asphyxiated by the bombs placed in the church.

It was different from the impersonal slaughter carried out by airmen from a great height. Tacticians and politicians have given reasons for Hiroshima and Nagasaki and I believe some excuse was presented for Dresden. But no one has been able to establish beyond doubt the reason for Oradour. The population had done nothing to merit the dreadful fate they suffered and nothing was achieved by the exercise.

Even the German concentration camps which accounted for the deaths of millions of people were operated by the Nazis for a purpose. Moreover they were not unique. Such camps have been set up in other times of strife—pens to put people in (and dispose of them) if they become a nuisance to one side or the other.

It could be argued that the airman who presses the bomb release resulting in the extermination of a large number of innocent women and children (ignoring the men for the moment) is as guilty as the SS men who slaughtered the screaming prisoners in Oradour church. The difference lies in consciousness of the crime.

Phosphorus dropped on Hamburg and napalm dropped on Vietnam

caused death to hundreds in a similarly agonizing form to that meted out by the SS at Oradour, who appeared to have fired to cripple and then burned their victims alive. But did the airmen ponder at all on the effect on human flesh of their releasing their missiles? They probably hoped they were destroying military targets or killing soldiers of the other side, shutting out of their minds any pictures of people running around screaming, their clothes and hair on fire as a result of the stuff dropped on them.

Some of the concentration camps have been preserved with their ghastly apparatus as memorials of the horrors that were carried out there. However, Belsen, the only one I have visited, seemed more like a pleasant public park than a scene of indescribable cruelty. True, one is appalled by the huge mounds labelled to the effect that several thousand people are buried under each of them and there are reminders of the awful scenes revealed at the time of the liberation through photographs in a museum at the entrance. But the impact was far removed from that of Oradour.

The other camps, with their gas chambers, ovens, etc., still visible, are undoubtedly more shocking. But these places were specifically designed execution sites, unlike Oradour which was converted within the space of a few hours from a pleasant, populated village to a smoking place of execution.

Why keep Oradour in ruins? Most of the other war-shattered places have been rebuilt. Why not Oradour?

English-born Raymond Carter writing in his book Le Scandale d'Oradour (Le Cercle d'Or) argues against the preservation of the ruins. Here are some of his points:

(1) One does not perpetuate the memory of a cancer victim with a picture of his cancer and a description of his agony on his tomb.

(2) The dead would not have wished for the ruins of their homes to be kept as showpieces. The ruins have been officially preserved under the label of 'historic site', fortunately not yet debased to a tourist centre but studiously preserved for the curious.

(3) The children of Oradour would have preferred that other children should play and enjoy life where they did before their moment of terror ended their existence.

(4) After the war, the Germans wanted to rebuild the village. The offer was refused. This should not have happened.

(5) When one visits the ruins it is not to pay homage to the dead but rather to examine the detailed dissection of the sadistic work of the SS.

(6) The ruins keep alive hatred for the Germans which should be forgotten in view of current Franco-German relations. Many French towns and villages are twinned with German places.

(7) The few survivors who live in the new village feel that the Beaux Arts have expelled them from their homes. They should have been rebuilt and they should have been allowed to return. They feel their roots are in the old village and not in the new one. If they had been rehoused at a distance from the ruins this feeling might not be so strong but they are daily faced with the pathetic reminder of their former existence.

There is much sense in what Raymond Carter says. Analysing my own feelings, I doubt whether I should have made the long journey to Oradour to see a memorial in a rebuilt village. The ruins are a unique showpiece. They arouse feelings of enormous pity and horror. One walks in reverence (or at least one should) in a place which is really one vast cemetery.

I have visited war cemeteries in France, Germany and the Far East. The Singapore one is the most impressive I have seen, particularly during one of the daily downpours when the whole place seems to be weeping. Yet such places cannot be compared with Oradour. The neatness of row upon row of identical headstones numbs any shock effect, although one is taken aback by the numbers involved.

Oradour presents only too clearly the full story of the deaths of 642 people. One might get a similar effect in a war cemetery if it were littered with the carcasses of tanks and aircraft, each labelled, 'Ten men died here . . . Three men burned alive in this . . .' etc.

The ruins do keep alive hatred against the men who carried out the massacre and, by association, with Germany. Unfortunately, the inscriptions on the tombs label the killers as Germans, overlooking the mixed nationality involved.

Tulle, and other scenes of atrocities carried out by the Das Reich Division in that region, have nothing to show like Oradour, so their stories tend to be forgotten. Oradour has earned an international reputation.

I can appreciate the feelings of the rehoused survivors because, as I have said, the old village is so much more attractive than the new. The ruins may not be blatantly advertised as a tourist centre, but on a fine day in August (the French holiday month) there are many tourists and I've no doubt that Oradour is featured in the itinerary of some coach trips.

The Beaux Arts can be criticized for preserving the corpse, for perpetuating the memory of the crime. They have done their best to keep the ruins in good order by surrounding them with a wall and locking them up at night. But one wonders how they will look in another 30 years. Many of the rusty utensils and other household articles which form part of the show may well have disintegrated or been lifted by souvenir hunters. The wall is easy to scale and a night patrol is unlikely.

There is a slight possibility—although they've left it rather late now—that the Government's attitude may drastically change and the ruins may be rebuilt after all. The carcases are of sound stone construction and should not be very difficult to restore. And I am sure that a new generation would not be averse to taking up residence in such a pleasant place.

SS Ranks with the British Army Equivalent

Oberstgruppenführer .... General
Obergruppenführer .... Lieut-General
Gruppenführer .... Major-General
Brigadeführer .... Brigadier
Oberführer and
  Standartenführer .... Colonel
Obersturmbannführer .... Lieut-Colonel
Sturmbannführer .... Major
Hauptsturmführer .... Captain
Obersturmführer .... Lieutenant
Untersturmführer 2nd-Lieutenant

(Joachim Kleist, the Gestapo man, had the title of Oberscharführer, which is equivalent to Sergeant-Major.)

Bibliography

Petite Histoire d'Oradour-sur-Glane—Albert Hivernaud.

Oradour-sur-Glane, Vision d'Epouvante—Guy Pachou et Dr Pierre Masfrand (Charles-Lavauzelle et Cie).

Trafics et Crimes Sous l'Occupation—Jacques Delarue (Fayard).

Crimes Ennemis en France, Oradour-sur-Glane (Archives du Service de Recherche des Crimes de Guerre Ennemis).

Dans l'Enfer d'Oradour—Pierre Poitevin (Société des Journaux et Publications du Centre, Limoges).

Le Scandale d'Oradour—Raymond Carter (Le Cercle d'Or)

Madness at Oradour—Jens Kruuse (Secker and Warburg).

The Waffen SS, Hitler's Elite Guard at War—George H. Stein (Oxford University Press).

Uniforms, Organisation and History of the Waffen SS—R. J. Bender and H. P. Taylor (Bender).

Waffen SS, Its Uniforms, Insignia and Equipment—D. S. V. Fosten and R. J. Marrion (Altmark Publications).

A Pictorial History of the Waffen SS 1923–44—Andrew Mollo (Macdonald and Jane's).

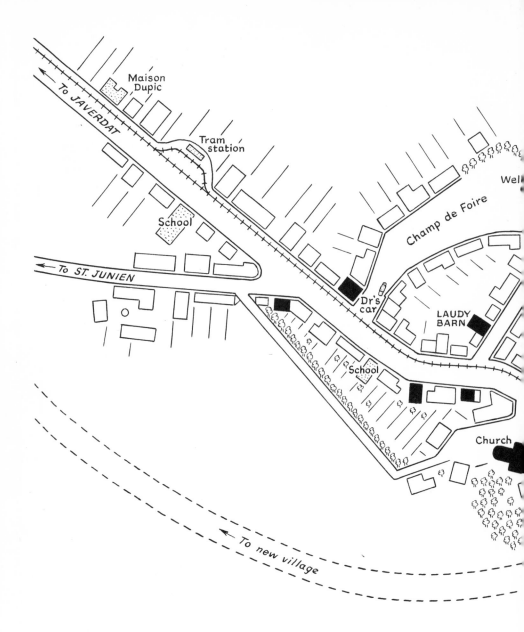

ORADOUR-SUR-GLANE

(Not to scale)